Coincidence or Godincidence

Stories of miracles, mysteries and hope

By

Steve Rose

with **Kathi Rose**

Winners Success Network Publishing
Neenah, Wisconsin

Coincidence or Godincidence
Stories of miracles, mysteries and hope
By Steve Rose with Kathi Rose

First Edition, first printing
©2005 by Steve and Kathi Rose

ISBN: 0-9666819-5-9 (trade paper)

We would like to acknowledge the many contributors who granted us written permission to publish their stories in this book.

Winners Success Network Publishing
Box 404
Neenah, WI 54957-0404
www.godincidencebook.com

Coincidence or Godincidence

Book idea, story discovery, research, titles and first drafts by Steve Rose
Story rewriting, editing, consulting and cover concept by Kathi Rose
Book cover graphic design by Jackie Johnson, Appleton, WI
Executive assistance to Steve Rose provided by Mike Utech
Back cover photo courtesy of Linda Jeschke, Daggett, MI
Printed in the USA at PrintSourcePlus, Appleton, WI

We dedicate this book to Sarah,
who is, by her very existence, a walking miracle.

She has brought a touch
of the divine to our lives
by being a living example of love,
forgiveness, and childlike faith.

Thanks for reminding us
that life is to be lived to its fullest
each and every day.
We love you.

Contents

Acknowledgements

We would like to acknowledge many special people who have helped us with this book. We owe a special thanks to Darlene and Dennis Wiegman, Pastor Dan Gibson and his wife, Debbie, and Benjamin Sasse. Not only are they the consummate cheerleaders for this project, but their fervent prayer helped birth this book. We also want to say thanks to Jackie Johnson who unselfishly lent her talents to this project.

Steve would like to recognize the men of his accountability group, Dan Kiefer, Gary Baltz, and Bob Gardinier. They remind him "iron truly does sharpen iron." Special thanks to his right-hand-man and trusted friend, Mike Utech, for "hanging in" through not only this challenge, but many others.

Last, but certainly not least, thanks to the many contributors whose stories submitted have made this book possible.

A note from the Publisher

While the Publisher cannot guarantee all the claims of the contributor, each contributor of the stories in this book has signed a release verifying his/her story to be true. The Publisher has done reasonable research and is satisfied they are valid and accurate, and feels confident that the events portrayed did indeed happen.

In many cases these stories speak for themselves, thus there is no "Story of the Story" following every chapter. For those that do include a "Story of the Story," it is because we felt a need to further clarify and elaborate.

The names in the stories have not been changed. The contributors offered to use their real names to further verify the authenticity of their stories. The publisher asks that, for the privacy of the contributors, you do not make any attempt to contact them directly, either via phone, mail or other mediums.

If you desire to contact a contributor or want additional story information, go to:

www.godincidencebook.com

Coincidence vs. Godincidence

by Steve Rose

Over coffee, friend and wise guy Roy Jacobsen once asked, "Steve, has it ever occurred to you that nothing ever "occurs" to God?" I thought about that for a moment. What a revelation, that nothing that *has* or *will* happen to anyone can catch God by surprise. Because we tend to think in human terms, it's natural to feel that God's not always paying attention to what's going on in our lives. There are some who would want to make the case that God "blinks." My wife would argue the point. (See *"The Last Word"*)

My personal experiences suggest that God does indeed work supernaturally-naturally. There is a difference between oddities and Godities. There is a difference between saying, "Oh, that's *odd*," a coincidence, or "Oh, that's *God*," a Godincidence, regarding unexplainable happenings. We hope to present an opportunity here to help you make up your own mind.

This book was birthed after a random meeting with a man I had never met before. We made small talk and then he asked me a question.

"What's your name?" he asked, extending his hand.

"Steve Rose," I said.

Suddenly he turned white!

"Are you the Steve Rose who was on WNAM Radio back in the mid '80s?" he quizzed.

"Yes, sir. What's your name?" I asked.

"Gary Beyer," he said. "I need to tell you why it's providential that we've bumped into each other today."

"My mother, Grace Beyer, was your biggest fan when you were on the radio. She used to call you all the time. Steve, she talked about you a lot, I mean that."

I recalled the days when this special woman would call me during my show, after having won a contest, or just to talk. She would always encourage and "love on me" a bit. I appreciated her so much.

Gary put his hand on his chin and then slowly said these words that I will never forget.

"Steve, I need to tell you that even though you've never met her, or probably hadn't thought about her for the last eighteen years, it is no coincidence that you should bump into me. My mother passed away at 1:15 this afternoon!"

Something about meeting me that day comforted Gary during his early stage of shock, and I was grateful to know that God had put Grace into my life for a time. This meeting apparently had something in it for each of us. This "Godincidence" was the one that led me to pray about writing this book.

Both my wife and I are suckers for a happy, hopeful ending, and each of the stories has one, although it may take faith to believe that. Many of these tales have challenged our common sense and stretched our faith. Perhaps they'll do the same for you. One thing that really disturbs both of us is when there are stories that clearly point toward "divine intervention," a miracle if you will, and it gets passed off as a "coincidence." We make the argument that these happenings are God's way of getting our attention, letting us know He is watching and cares deeply about each and everyone of us.

So, before you get lost in this book we have one more question. "Is the fact you are holding this book coincidence or Godincidence?"

Lifeguards on Duty

Seventy-one percent of the earth's surface is water. Seventy-five percent of the human body is made up of water, also. If one thirsts, it can refresh. On a hot summer day a pool of it can be cooling. Caught in a moving ocean of it, however, can be deadly. Just ask Mark and Jill Abram, and a few of their friends.

In July of 1999, Mark Abram and several teenagers from his church youth group were in Tijuana, Mexico, on a servant event. As was the tradition on these trips, the entire group of thirty spent Sunday afternoon swimming and body surfing in the Pacific Ocean on Rosa Rita Beach. Public access was about a half-mile long and there were houses with a beautiful scenic view of the area all along the beachfront.

On this particular day, July 18, Mark brought the students, including his sixteen-year-old daughter, Jill, to the beach. The four-to-five foot waves were providing plenty of fun and frolic. Five of the young men and Jill headed for the water. Mark would join them shortly, but before they ran for the adventure of the waves, he had a warning.

"Be careful, you guys, and watch out for the undertow."

"We will," they assured him as they headed for the enticing waves.

Mark felt confident there was no undertow because the current seemed to be pulling north, across the beach, rather than out into the open water. Just a few minutes later Mark joined the six in the water. Thanks to an extensive sandbar, they were in only four feet of water about fifty feet from the shore.

"Watch this, Dad!" Jill yelled above the crashing waves as she displayed her body surfing skills.

"Wow, that was great!" dad yelled back to her.

Typically, the kids were able to ride a wave for five seconds, but it could carry them at least ten or fifteen feet. The playfulness continued for about 20 minutes when the sandbar shifted suddenly, and then disappeared. Gleeful laughter immediately was replaced by a piercing scream from one of the boys!

"I can't touch the bottom!" he yelled.

Soon the other five also found themselves over their heads in water with sizeable waves no longer under their bodies, but crashing on top of them. Not only were there huge swells, but they were also accompanied by powerful undertows that were pulling each of them further and further from the beach.

Two of the boys who were strong swimmers were able to reach shore, but just barely. Now a couple minutes into the panic, Mark swam over to Jill, who was quite frightened and near exhaustion.

"Honey, grab on," said the daddy who had come to the rescue of his little girl.

It became apparent immediately just how exhausted and spent she really was. He began to support both of them, but it became obvious that he couldn't possibly fight the undertow for both of them and keep them afloat for long. Suddenly he began to experience a wide range of emotions and thoughts in the flash of just a few moments.

"I don't wanna die!" surfaced in his thoughts. Then he was confronted with an eerie calm of, "We are going to die." Along with the sickening feeling came another realization. This beach didn't believe in having lifeguards. Mark could see hundreds of people on the beach helplessly watching their ordeal. Without a miracle, and there didn't appear to be any on the horizon, they were clearly headed for death.

As another large swell buried them deeper below the surface and pushed them further out to open water, other thoughts now passed through Mark's mind in rapid-fire progression.

"What a silly way to die," was his first thought. Then came, "What will happen to my family? How will they react to the loss of both Jill and me?" And finally, morbidly, "Which one of the two of us will drown first?" he wondered.

Their battle for survival seemed to last an hour, but incredibly it had been ongoing for only approximately four minutes. Still, he had no more strength left in him to fight the battle. It was then his eyes caught an unbelievable sight. Could he be seeing things? Paddling out to them was a lifeguard! Behind him were two more, each wearing baggy red shorts.

The first lifeguard reached him and Jill in the nick of time. Their fatigue coupled with the strength of the current was just too much for them. The other two lifeguards went past Mark and Jill to rescue the other three kids who had been pulled out into even deeper water. Mark struggled to convince himself that they would survive even now. His opinion changed somewhat when he saw that the powerful swimmer was wearing fins. Attached to his left hand was about a six-foot rope pulling a red float, similar to a boogie board.

The lifeguard motioned for them to grab the float. Mark decided to try to help the rescue by kicking along with the lifeguard. It appeared the young man did not speak any English, so it was difficult for him to convey to Mark that he did not want Mark's help whatsoever. A kind of glare helped Mark realize the man wanted to do the work. Mark's and Jill's job was to simply hold on and stay calm, so that's exactly what they did.

Within moments they were on the shore where they collapsed in a heap. Soon the other three boys had found sand as well, thanks to the young men who had risked their lives to get them from what seemed to be a certain watery grave. Many of the spectators on the beach watched them as they coughed and tried to catch their breath. Each of them was trying to process what had really just happened.

Approximately fifteen minutes after the rescue, Mark could see a four-wheeler coming toward them from further up the beach where the rest of his group was. Driving the vehicle was the very same lifeguard who had just saved him and his daughter. The lifeguard pulled up right next to them. Unable to speak English, he motioned to them to get in the small vehicle. They hopped aboard. He took them back to their group who were waiting about two hundred yards south from where they had been rescued.

Jill got off and ran to her waiting friends. Mark looked at this young warrior who had unequivocally saved their lives. Everything up until this point suggested to Mark that there was a language barrier between them and the lifeguards. So, Mark motioned to him as if to be peeling cash from his hand and into the lifeguard's. What he heard next was more than perplexing. It was astonishing.

The lifeguard shook his head as if to suggest, "No, thank-you," and then through a smile on his face, with perfect English said, "I'm just doing my job."

"Thank you so much," said Mark as he extended his hand to him in gratitude.

Soon the lifeguard was gone from his sight, heading back down the beach. Mark spent some time with the group of kids before feeling compelled to go back down the beach to thank the men once more for their acts of heroism.

Down the sandy ground he went. He tried to communicate with those congregated near the water that he was looking for the lifeguards. He pointed out to the open seas, trying to let them know that he was one of the men who had been saved just an hour earlier. Other hand gestures and motions were failing as well.

"If anything, I'll see the little red floats," he thought to himself, still confident he would find the three lifeguards on duty somewhere along the beach.

Mark continued to try to communicate with the onlookers on the beach, but they all seemed very standoffish and very confused by what he was trying to suggest, that he was looking for the lifeguards. He was determined that he would not go back to his group until he had thanked these people one more time.

The response was the same, confusion and silence. It was at this time that Mark became overwhelmed with emotion. Tears began to drip from below his sunglasses. Something about this entire event was very peculiar. What may have actually just taken place was occurring to him. It took a little bit of extra work and investigation, but finally Mark got his answer and, at last, the chapter was closed. He knew his life would be changed forever.

Upon further review, and gleaned information from those in the know in the area who did speak English, he learned that not only were there no lifeguards at Rosa Rita Beach that Sunday in July of 1999, but there had never been lifeguards there—ever!

Our Daily Cereal

In 1982 Pat and Linda Boyer were experiencing both growing and hunger pains. They were a couple in their late 20s working as in-state missionaries for Youth For Christ. As part of this magnificent calling, it was their humbling task to raise their own funds on which to live. It wasn't unusual to go through dry spells, but during one challenging season food was scarce in the cupboard and supplies were dwindling in the refrigerator. It was during one of these times for the Boyers that "childlike faith" got their attention. The other member in the Boyer home was little Christi, Linda's and Pat's six-year-old who one day had a request.

"Daddy, can I have cereal for breakfast tomorrow?" she asked. He didn't quite know how to tell her, but he knew he needed to answer.

"Baby, we don't have any."

Quite honestly, Pat was angry with God. He thought, "God you've asked us to be your servants. Here we are with little money and my daughter wants only cereal and we don't have any." He was not a happy camper, but the little girl was determined to have cereal in the morning and she had a plan to get it.

"Daddy, can we pray to God for some cereal?"

Although he didn't say it, Pat thought, "Yeah, sure, like it's going to do any good. God can't even get us a paycheck. If He did we'd have cereal."

Needless to say, his faith had dwindled to the level of nourishment in their home. So he did what any "doubting dad" would do, and that was to allow his daughter, who didn't know any better than to fully trust God, to be the one to pray for the need of the moment.

"Sweetheart, why don't you pray," he told her. So she did.

"Dear Jesus," she began. "We don't have any cereal in our house and I want some tomorrow. So please bring us some cereal, Amen," she finished.

Pat was grinning inside while almost sarcastically challenging God to prove his ability to provide. Admittedly, he did find it cute to observe the faith his daughter expressed, which had not come from him, at least not at the moment.

"Alright, it's time for bed," he said.

In a few minutes Christi was sound asleep.

The Boyers awoke to a beautiful autumn morning. He did think of little Christi's prayer the night before. The thought made him both laugh and cry at the same time. He decided to poke his head out the front door to see what the weather was like. As he did so, his eyes caught the sight of a bag sitting in front of the door. He had no idea who had left it there. As he stooped down to pick it up, what he found inside the bag would not only warm his heart, but would also give him a sermon that he now tells to whoever will listen.

Inside the bag were a few grocery items. Better yet, there was $100 in cash that would pay a few bills. He pulled out a couple of cans and a few boxes of dry goods. Still, there was something else at the bottom of the bag. As Dad pulled the last item to the top of the bag he began to weep. Only the power of the prayer of a little girl could have left him holding what Christi had prayed for just hours earlier—a box of cereal!

The Story of the Story

Steve heard this story directly from Pat. Twenty-three years later the details of it still make Pat cry. He can't recall what kind of cereal it was, but he's pretty sure it was actually the exact brand that Christi had asked for!

Gimme Some Kind of Sign, God!

Jean Harder was having a bad day. Just two months earlier, in August of '03, she and her husband Paul had dropped their son Aaron off at the University of Wisconsin-Milwaukee as a college freshman. She had dropped their daughter Andrea off at Concordia three years earlier. Now she was officially an "empty nester" and not handling it well at all on this particular crisp October day.

Jean decided to take a trip to Appleton. One of the goals for the day was to go to The Learning Shop to purchase some supplies for the library for her home church, St. Luke's Lutheran. She had a recurring question that kept bouncing around rather loudly in her mind since early that morning.

"God, do you love me?" she asked.

She knew the answer, but asked the question anyway.

Jean wandered through the store until she found what she needed, then made her way back to her 1994 blue Geo. Jean was struggling with an overflow of love for her children and nowhere to deposit it. Yes, she loved God. Yes, she could pour her love out to Him, but would it be enough to satisfy the longing and loneliness she was feeling? And did He really love her? Could He love her in a way that was tangible to her?

She unlocked the car door and started the engine. The radio began playing a song that reminded her of Aaron and brought tears to her eyes. Again, she found herself asking if God was enough. She was prepared to pull out of the driveway of the store and take a left onto Casaloma Drive when, across the way, a dark green van was attempting to pull out from Fazoli's parking lot to take a right on the same road. Jean waited for him.

In the time it took to wait for the van to pull out, Jean Harder quietly told God, "I know you love the world, but God, today I, Jean Harder, need to know that you love *me*!" The van finally pulled out into the right lane. She pulled out into the inside lane. The green vehicle was about fifteen feet ahead of her on the right when she saw the most incredible sight that she has ever seen. She gazed at a personalized state of Wisconsin Department of Motor Vehicle license plate. It read:

LVUJEAN

The Story of the Story

Tom Balliew from the singing group "The Voices of Peace" suggested Steve call Jean Harder when he heard about our plans to write the book. When Steve connected with Jean via the phone he found an enthusiasm that was contagious! There is no question her experience has changed her life.

They discussed her "faith mystery miracle" and how they could possibly find the person with the license plate. She admitted she had considered doing that in the past, but never had. As they chatted, Steve felt led to ask her how she reacted when she saw the plate. He assumed maybe she cried harder. Just the opposite occurred. She said she laughed so hard for nearly five minutes that she nearly ran off the road!

Here are a couple additional and significant facts to the story. First, she could have pulled out in front of the van, but she didn't, she let him pull out first. Second, since this experience she no longer signs her personal letters, "Love Jean," but "Love you, Jean." To her there's a big difference, at least since that day when she was looking for a sign—and she got it.

Wake Me at 3:53

Sheila and Chuck Loehr are an average married couple. Sheila, a woman full of life, can brighten a room just by entering it. Chuck is an equally likeable, somewhat reserved, "blue collar" kind of fellow who works and plays hard. They married on February 3, 1973. It's fair to say they are quite different from one another and have had more than their share of marital difficulties, not unlike thousands of other couples that have made the same covenant, "to have and to hold until death do us part."

On Saturday, June 7, 1997, Chuck and Sheila gathered at the American Club for an extended family function on Sheila's side. There was fun, frolic, and dancing. One of the guests attending the gathering was Julie Palomares. It didn't take Julie long to notice that the usually bubbly Sheila was not her usual self. Julie had decided she would attempt to find a quiet place where she could spend some quality, quiet time with Sheila. She spotted a lonely hallway with a gorgeous grand piano at the end of it and encouraged Sheila to join her there.

"Sheila, what's the matter?" she asked.

It took only seconds for Sheila to begin to weep and pour her heart out to Julie.

"I heard on the radio talk show today that God doesn't want us to lie and I feel like my entire marriage is nothing but a lie. Chuck and I have nothing in common. I just feel like I'm living a lie. I'm not in love with him," she confessed. "I'm tired of living like this."

Sheila's confession had not caught Julie by surprise. Having known Sheila and Chuck for as long as she had, and having heard Sheila's heart, Julie did what good friends do and that was to be a good listener. She paused before giving counsel to her friend.

"Sheila, remember God loves you. He knows your situation better than you do. He cares about the pain you are in. You can trust Him to take the difficult challenges of your life, including your marriage, and bring good from them," she paused and then continued.

"Could I pray for you and Chuck?"

"Yeah, of course," agreed Sheila fighting back another deluge of tears.

With clasped hands, closed eyes and bowed heads Julie began to speak aloud. The humble woman of faith, who had watched God powerfully answer prayers in her own life, prayed that He would show himself in a mighty way to them.

"Lord, you know the plans you have for Chuck's and Sheila's lives. Lord, I pray for them to have what Jesus died to give them. Speak to each of their hearts. We take authority over the enemy of our souls and the way he has tried to destroy this marriage. Give Chuck grace to love Sheila as Christ loves the church. Give Sheila wisdom, no matter how Chuck decides to live his life. Help her to know what to do, what to say and how to say it to him. *You* are the One who restores, so we trust *You* to intervene in their lives. We thank *You* and give *You* all the glory for what *You* are going to do in this situation. In Jesus' name we pray, Amen."

Sheila looked up at Julie with tear-brimmed eyes. Julie had some simple words of comfort and encouragement to share with Sheila before they parted.

"The Lord is good, Sheila, and He will take care of you, no matter what." Then she looked into the eyes of her friend and made a bold statement, "Sheila, I really believe God is going to do something wonderful for you. Can you believe that?"

"Yes," responded a weary-looking Sheila.

When she returned to the party, Sheila noticed that Chuck was still planted in the same place he had been when she had left with Julie, standing at the bar chatting with friends. Sheila decided she would have as much fun as she could under the circumstances, so she danced her heart out and mingled with friends.

The events of the evening came to an end. The Loehrs began the one-hour drive home in what felt like a deafening silence for the first fifteen minutes. Having had a few cans of courage, the usually agreeable, somewhat quiet Chuck broke the silence. He had something to say to his wife of twenty-four years.

"You know, after tonight I'm convinced now, more than ever, that you and I are not compatible at all. We want different things," said Chuck. "We really don't belong together."

Sheila was unusually calm and not surprised by what Chuck was saying. As a matter of fact, she agreed with him. Although her faith was challenged when she heard Julie pray for them just a few hours prior asking for God "to move" on behalf of their marriage, Sheila realized there simply was no fight left in her. Chuck took a deep breath and then continued.

"I think we need to separate," he blurted out. "We'll move into separate bedrooms for now and then see where it goes from there, but I've pretty much had it with us," he confessed.

"All right," agreed Sheila, as quiet resignation seemed to seep into the depth of her soul.

Upon arriving home, Chuck made his way upstairs, changed clothes, then came back down to nestle into his recliner. Sheila slept in what had been just a few hours earlier "their" bedroom. Chuck nodded off and on while Sheila tossed and turned, processing the decision Chuck had made earlier. Barring a miracle, they were headed for divorce.

The sunlight was gently spreading its rays into the room and across Sheila's face at 6:10 the following morning. Suddenly she became aware of someone standing next to her bed. It was Chuck. Through her own tired, swollen and weepy eyes, Sheila immediately noticed that Chuck's eyes looked different.

"What do you want?" she asked wondering what he could possibly have to say after last night's conversation.

"Sheila, I've come up here to ask you to forgive me for not being the husband I'm supposed to be. I'm sorry that I haven't loved you as Christ loves the church."

Sheila was utterly startled and astounded by what she was hearing. Chuck was speaking word for word what Julie had prayed aloud just hours earlier! Specifically, Julie had prayed that Chuck would love Sheila as Christ loved the church and that God would help him to become the husband that God wanted him to be. Now here was Chuck confessing to Sheila the very prayer Julie had invoked last night!

This was certainly nothing short of miraculous. Sheila recalled that Julie said, "God's going to do something for you." How amazing that God would answer Julie's prayer so quickly! The stunned wife had just one question for her husband who had clearly had some kind of revelation or awakening.

"Chuck, what in the world has happened to you?"

"Sheila," he gulped. "I'm not sure you'll be able to believe this, but an angel woke me up at 3:53. He told me to come and tell you this!"

If a Purse Could Talk

Kristin Pynenberg stood by the side of the Little Chute swimming pool. She wanted to jump into the nearby Fox River and simply float away. She was absolutely "heart sick" and her stomach wasn't doing much better because of what she had allowed to happen. Now, only minutes into living a too-true-to-life nightmare, she also came to the conclusion that this moment was *not* the time to start rehearsing her regrets over the situation. It was, however, the time to pray. That's certainly what it was going to take to redeem and restore her current dilemma.

It was mid-afternoon of August 2, 2005, when Kristin and her two sisters, her brother and friend had gone to the Little Chute swimming pool in Doyle Park. They found a place against the wire fence in the pool area where they could set their belongings. Kristin, 18, put her purse behind another one already there. She then joined everyone else for some fun in the water.

At around 5 p.m. the crowd had thinned out to just a few dozen people because it was time to close the pool for the day. As Kristin arrived at the spot where they had set down their belongings, her heart nearly burst out of her chest, and she then let out a cry of helplessness.

"Oh, my goodness, my purse is gone!" she exclaimed with a panic-filled voice.

It had not been out of her sight for long. The other purse that had been sitting in front of Kristin's earlier that day, quite strangely, was still there.

As panic set in, Kristin noticed her Aunt Erin was bringing her cousin for swimming lessons.

"Are you sure you put it there, Kristin?"

"Yeah, oh my God!"

After a brief search, there seemed to be little hope they would find her purse or its contents. It was now after 5 p.m., so it was too late to call the banks to protect her from any unauthorized charges that could be made on her missing checkbook. Kristin called her mother, Heidi, who arrived on the scene very quickly.

"We need to call the police," said a take-charge Heidi.

Kristin was becoming ill at the thought of what had been in her purse that was now surely gone. A haunting thought tortured her mind when she recalled that she had initially contemplated leaving her purse in her car, but then reconsidered when she realized that she'd need it if she was going to buy some treats for the kids.

Policeman Jim Brandt, from the Little Chute Police Department, arrived on the scene to get all the details of the missing purse.

"Kristin, can you describe your purse and everything that was in it?" he questioned.

"Well," she gulped. "I had about $100 worth of gift certificates from Gordman's, four other certificates from Best Buy, some free movie passes from the Regal Cinemas and my cell phone," she began.

"Anything else?"

She sighed and continued. "It had my keys, my watch (which was a keepsake from her mom) and my I.D. from UW-Stevens Point. Both of my checkbooks were in there along with bank cards and my driver's license."

Then came the worst news of all. Kristin hesitated for a moment then went on.

"And, uh, I had about $100 in cash in it," she confessed as her voice trailed off.

After she got home she realized there was actually $400 in cash. She had forgotten about the tithe money she had tucked away and the money her mom had paid her for two months of babysitting.

An unofficial tally put the value of the missing contents at nearly $1,000! Now Kristin wanted to cry. Soon the family had disbursed from the pool. One of the first things Heidi did was to help her daughter make a list of all the places she would have to call the next day to cancel accounts, get a new driver's license, and gift certificates. Heidi immediately called her boyfriend, Don, to cancel the cell phone. Don, a strong believer in the power of prayer, immediately offered the situation to God.

At dinner that evening the family gathered for prayer. Each person at the table was touched by what had happened and hearts were heavy. Prayers were offered for the person who had taken the purse and also that the Lord would be glorified by the situation.

Heidi's sister, Erin, spread the word to friends and others from the church. She called family members and gathered her children to pray.

Soon the heavenlies would be bombarded with requests for Kristin to find the missing purse. What's even more impressive was everyone was encouraged to pray specifically that whoever took the purse would feel remorse for what he had done and would return it to Kristin.

At 10:14 p.m., Heidi's sister and Kristin's aunt, Erin Hietpas, e-mailed Pastor Mike Collison to tell him that her niece had lost her purse containing hard-earned money she had saved to attend her first year of college that fall. There was also an affirmation in it.

Erin wrote, "Heidi and Kristin are two women of faith. I guess I want to pray that they will remain hopeful and remember that the Lord provides for those who believe Him and are obedient to Him."

Is prayer powerful? Well, as far as this case is concerned, you can determine for yourself. The following Wednesday evening, August 3 at 9:43 p.m., Erin sent out an e-mail of celebration.

Erin wrote, " I just got a phone call from my niece. A man turned in her purse to the Little Chute police department. Nearly everything was in it, except her cell phone. What an AWESOME God we serve!" she professed.

What had happened? Well, about 100-yards from the swimming pool runs the murky Fox River. It seems a fisherman, nearly a mile away from the pool in Heesacker Park, had barely dropped his hook into the water when he felt something on the end of his line. It was heavy, but not putting up any type of fight.

Yes, he had indeed caught something, but it certainly didn't feel like a fish. He knew from the lack of "tug" that something was different. He gave another jerk to his line. He couldn't believe what popped to the surface. In an unbelievable, one-in-a-million snag, there, hooked on the end of his line, was Kristin's purse!

The Story of the Story

Kristin would be the first to admit that it was seemingly irresponsible to be carrying around such a "valuable" purse. Because her folks were divorced, and she lived in two houses throughout the week, her purse became her central location for everything important to her.

In the process of this experience, Kristin, a naive, small-town girl, learned a valuable lesson to prepare her for going away to college that fall.

This is just another story of God's willingness to redeem our mistakes when our hearts are right. Kristin had tucked away some money that she was planning to tithe to her church. Kristin believed in the Biblical principle of giving 10% of her income to the church. That money was still in the purse when it was found.

It is still the family's prayer that someday they may meet and forgive whoever it was that took Kristin's purse. Too bad a purse can't talk. What a story it could tell!

From Another Plane

By mid-morning, Friday, March 10 of 1989, the work week was over for project manager Ron Mandich, 52, and two co-workers. They had just finished a three-week machine rebuild in Dryden, Ontario, Canada, for Valmet Paper Machinery.

It was noon as the men sat on the runway of Pearson International Airport in a Fokker F-28. Aboard the same flight were 65 passengers and a crew of four. Every seat was occupied. Ron was in aisle seat 8-C on the left side of the plane. The left side of the plane had sets of three seats; the right had sets of two. It was 32 degrees and a heavy snow was falling steadily. Captain George Morwood came over the intercom with an announcement.

"Folks, we're waiting for a small Cessna to land and then we'll depart for Winnipeg. We should be in the air shortly. Thank you for your patience, and enjoy the flight," he said.

At 12:11 p.m., Air Canada flight #1363 sped down the runway, reaching a lift-off speed of nearly 150 mph, struggling to become airborne. Suddenly its wheels hit the runway with a thud. Something was clearly not right, but the plane had reached the "point of no return." There was a substantial drop off at the end of the runway so another touchdown was not going to work. Ron heard the sound of the engines go full throttle. The plane finally did lift to about 15-feet above the runway. From the trajectory of the plane and its inability to gain proper altitude over the densely wooded area, it became obvious immediately to attendant Sonia Hartwick, who was seated across the aisle from Ron, that the flight was in serious trouble!

"Assume the "brace" position. The plane is going to crash!" she cried out.

For Ron Mandich, it was time to have what he assumed might be his last conversation, on this side of eternity, with his heavenly Father.

"Well, Lord, this may be the day I meet you face-to-face," he prayed calmly.

Deep within he sensed an inaudible voice say, "You will survive."

He leaned forward in anticipation of the crash. There was no time for fear to manifest itself. Ron remembers the thought quickly passing through his mind that, one way or another, it would all be over in a matter of seconds.

There was a thunderous noise as the plane was rocked and jolted from the impact of the hundreds of treetops that were ripping away at the undercarriage of the fuselage.

Ron remembers his arms, legs and head flailing wildly from the violent trauma. The airplane jerked and shuddered as it began to hit the tops of the trees and slam and rip into the trunks of the trees. Inexplicably, he stayed belted in his seat. The sound of the plane hitting the trees was indescribably loud and traumatic. The trees, approximately six to ten inches in diameter, gutted the belly of the fuselage, sheared the left wing completely off and mangled the right one as the plane rolled counter-clockwise. Fuel began to spill and spray from the decimated aircraft to the ground below and into the passenger compartment.

Deafening screams resounded throughout the cabin. The out-of-control plane cut a quarter-mile long and one-hundred-foot-wide swath through the dense stand of trees. Thankfully, as the plane plunged into the forest, there was a slight decline to the terrain that allowed for more of a downhill slide rather than a direct impact with the ground. After flying a little less than six-tenths of a mile from the end of the runway in less than fifteen seconds, the plane had crashed into the wooded area, landing in about three to four feet of snow. Lives were snuffed out in that moment of impact, but Ron Mandich's was not one of them. Miraculously, he sustained no life threatening injuries from the crash.

Although he was shaken, once he got his bearings, he could see fire and smell smoke, but was unaware that some of the passenger seats were burning. Ron couldn't see anyone else in the plane. The windows in the airplane were small and did not permit much light to enter. He knew that he needed to escape, and quickly! In the heavy smoke around him he noticed light emanating from an opening a few rows up on the right side of the wreckage.

Ron knew he needed to go to it, but he first had to get out of his seat. He reached to unbuckle his seat belt, but there was no seatbelt buckle to be found. He reached to his left, no buckle. He felt in the middle, no buckle. He felt to his right, still no buckle. In a moment of inspiration he reached with his right hand around behind the seat and found it. The seat had torn loose from the floor and slid forward, causing the seat belt buckle to slide through the seat bottom and backrest. He was able to reach around his seat and find the seat belt buckle and release it with one hand.

It was time to move. The opening he had spotted earlier on the right side was several rows forward. The hole was football-shaped, about four feet high from top to bottom and two-and-a-half feet wide. He proceeded to make his way forward. Suddenly, he felt extreme heat on his face and involuntarily recoiled. That surge of searing heat forced him back to the far left of the plane! Amazingly, he felt no fear. Intuitively he understood maintaining a sense of urgency was his only chance to stay alive.

"I either go out that hole or I am going to die," he said to himself.

Ron quietly prayed under his breath. He could smell the stench of the fuel-soaked seats all around him. His engineering background taught him that he could go through fire if he passed through it quickly enough. He stepped up onto the armrest of the left side aisle seat facing the large hole. Taking the starting position of a racing swimmer, he coiled his body and then dove headfirst through the flames and out of the hole. He landed in a heap into the cold snow, a startling and sobering change from just a split second before. He received scratches and bruises to his stomach and chest and a cracked rib from a broken tree stump he had landed on, but he was alive. Ron had taken a leap of faith to survival! Twenty-four others would not be as fortunate.

Having exited the inferno, he now could hear many others who had escaped out the back of the airplane calling for him to get away from the wreckage before it blew. He began to trudge through the deep snow toward them when, suddenly, there was a muffled voice coming from behind him.

"He-e-elp me," he heard.

Ron turned around and saw a hand sticking out of the snow next to the airplane, just a hand. He trudged back toward the airplane, grabbed the hand and pulled with all his might. Snow flew in every direction as a man's body appeared! Together they made their way to safety. Rescue vehicles arrived and Ron was admitted to the hospital for six hours of waiting and observation. His wife, Mary Anne, was contacted by a local pastor to inform her that Ron had survived and was doing well. Valmet, Ron's employer, chartered a plane and picked up Ron and only one of the two other men in Dryden. Tragically, the other gentleman was one of the twenty-four that died.

Within a week of the crash, the C.A.S.B. (Canadian Air Safety Board) sent someone to Ron's home to interview him. So into a tape recorder he spoke, detailing what you have read here.

On September 25, 1989, Ron and about half of the survivors convened in Thunder Bay for an inquiry hearing. One of the lawyers for the Crash Inquiry Committee asked if he could speak with Ron privately.

"Sir, we'd like to talk to you about what you are going to say when you get on the stand."

"Sure," said the mild-mannered Mandich.

Ron was escorted to a small room off to the side.

"Mr. Mandich, in the taped testimony you gave to the representative of the C.A.S.B. at your home shortly after the crash, you spoke of a 'gaping hole' that you dove out of on the right side of the plane somewhere around rows five and six, correct?"

"That's right," he affirmed.

"Mr. Mandich, we called Ottawa where they are currently storing the plane in a hangar. There is no hole in the side of the plane!" he reported. "However, we don't want you to feel badly. Four others reported that they escaped out of the same hole!"

The Story of the Story

Of the twenty-one passengers sitting in front of Ron in Row 8 on the left side of the airplane, only two survived—one passenger in Row 7, and, oddly, one in Row 2. No one behind Row 8 died and only two passengers on the right side of the aisle died. Both pilots and the stewardess seated in the jump seat behind the cockpit also died. The stewardess seated across from Ron was the only member of the crew to survive.

In the time that the plane sat at the boarding gate and on the runway waiting for the Cessna to land, ice built up on the cold wings. Icing alters and degrades the lift characteristics of the wing. In the final analysis, that's what doomed Air Canada flight #1363.

Here's a somewhat humorous note. Ron had a pair of warm brown boots in his suitcase on the flight. While he was at the hospital he spotted them in the hallway. Someone explained that his suitcase was found and the boots were given to the surviving stewardess, Sonia Hartwick, since she had lost her high-heeled shoes in her escape. Ron showed Steve those boots. He also still has the shoes he was wearing that propelled him to safety from the mangled, burning fuselage.

Baby on a Blanket

Summers are wonderful and much anticipated in the Upper Peninsula of Michigan. After months of snow and cold one doesn't miss opportunities to bask in the summer sun. Kathi Krieg was one such person. It was a daily ritual to take her 10-month old son, Nathan, out onto the small front lawn of her tiny rented home. Together they would lie stomach down on a blanket where she would read aloud to him until he fell asleep for his afternoon nap.

Next door was an elderly woman, Ethel, who was out each afternoon at the same time sweeping her front porch and sidewalk. It wasn't unusual for Ethel to glance toward her neighbor's front yard and chat with Kathi and check on Nathan, but on this particular day, she seemed preoccupied with her daily routine. Kathi continued to read aloud as Nathan drifted off to sleep.

Suddenly a man standing at the edge of the blanket appeared to Kathi. He was incredibly handsome, beautiful if you will. He had on a business suit and was wearing a look of concern on his face. He gazed down at Kathi and then spoke to her with an air of authority.

"Pick up the baby and move, now!"

Kathi felt compelled to obey his order. She dropped the book, leaned over and picked up Nathan immediately. She walked with a sense of urgency just 10 feet back and to the right corner of the house, and stood on the steps to her front door.

In what seemed like only an instant later, a rickety old pickup truck came around the corner too quickly and lost control. In a flash, the truck hopped the curb and suddenly stopped—right on top of the blanket where mom and baby had just been!

Obviously, there was now a mother who was in shock pondering the "what if" she had just witnessed. Within seconds Ethel from next door was on-site and also standing just feet away from what should have been a sure tragedy. She had seen the whole thing.

"Honey, are you and your baby all right?" she asked in a panicked tone.

"Yes, we're fine," Kathi replied in stunned but grateful disbelief. "Did you see that?" she asked her neighbor.

"Yes, I did, everything. Are you sure you're all right? How is Nathan?" who was now wide awake and stirring in her arms.

"Honestly, we're both just fine," she said now beginning to shake. Moments later Kathi had one more question.

"Ethel, where did the man go?"

The woman had just one short answer.

"What man?"*

The Story of the Story

By the way, this story is far from over...read the next story!

A Letter to Tanya

by Steve Rose

Juda High School was the next stop on my book tour. I arrived in town the night before I was scheduled to speak.

After a restful night, I awoke to a crisp, clear morning. It was October 22, 1997. At about 9:15 a.m. I made my way to the high school to present my message, *"The Power of Purpose."*

"Life is a gift, ladies and gentlemen," I began. "Live your life as if today could be your last," I encouraged.

I went on to tell them the "Billy Strassburg" story, who was one of my classmates. Billy was great looking, prom king, my friend, and one of the stars on the basketball team. He was tragically killed in a car accident at 16 years old on June 16, 1976.

After I closed my presentation, I was approached by one of the teachers, Jackie Klar. We chatted casually for a few moments before she extended an invitation to speak to her class. That was a no-brainer. After trying to keep the attention of a hundred students, now I would be able to keep eye contact with only fifteen or so.

The class and I had a wonderful time together. Inexplicably, my eyes kept drifting to the left side of the room, to a student named Tanya. She wore glasses, had blonde hair and a cheerful smile. As I spoke, I would direct a question to Tanya and tease her about her answer. She was being a great sport about it all.

After class, I thanked Tanya for allowing me to "pick on her." I then did something I rarely do. I gave a copy of one of my books to one individual from a group. I told the students that Tanya had been a good sport. They agreed she was a good choice. I said my farewells and left for my next engagement.

Three months after the Juda presentation, I received a short note from Jackie Klar wondering how my friends on the Packers were holding up after the Super Bowl loss. Her note reminded me of the day with her students. For some reason I felt compelled to send a card to Tanya. I summoned Mrs. Klar's help via a phone call to her home.

"Jackie, I feel that I'm to write a note to the young lady in your class named Tanya. Is there any way I could send you a note and have you make sure she gets it?"

"Let's do this," she wisely suggested. "So that your letter won't get lost at school, why not just send it to her home?"

I agreed this would be fine if she felt it was appropriate.

"Steve, I don't make a practice of providing this information, but I feel the need, in this situation, to honor your request. I know a note would encourage Tanya. Here's the address you're looking for," she said. I wrote as she spoke, checking the accuracy by reading it back to her.

The following Sunday, after church, I took a few minutes to send a note to Tanya. Frankly, I never thought about it again until March 31 when I came home from the office mid-morning to find a voice message on my answering machine.

"Steve, this is Jackie Klar. We've had a tragedy. You remember Tanya DeVoe? She just got her driver's license about nine weeks ago. This Sunday she was killed in a car accident. You can imagine we're a mess down here," she said crying. "But, mainly I thought you should know that Tanya talked a lot about the card you sent her. Anyway, I knew you'd want to know. God bless you, Steve. Bye."

Over the next few days my mind kept wandering back, remembering the school in that tiny community, the students, the family and a young woman whose earthly work was over. On the morning of Thursday, April 2, I knew I needed to go to Juda.

I phoned Juda High hoping I'd be able to talk with Jackie. They said she was right outside the office! She explained that visitation for Tanya was to be held that very afternoon. I said I'd be down by mid-afternoon.

By 4:45 p.m., I was pulling into the parking lot of the Newcomer Funeral Home in Monroe, which is just down the road from Juda. My heart pounded in anticipation of what was to come. I talked to a few of the students who were congregated in the parking lot. Then I greeted Tim, Jackie's husband, before making my way into the funeral home.

I knew it would be a long trip back home, so I hoped I could be one of the first ones to pay my respects.

While waiting in line I viewed a board of pictures of Tanya. Something was quite peculiar. The pictures suggested Tanya must have changed somewhat over the five and one-half months since I had seen her. She *must* have dyed her hair darker and lost some noticeable weight. She wasn't wearing glasses in any of the pictures either. "Maybe she had switched to contact lenses?" I wondered.

As I got closer to her casket I felt incredibly uncomfortable. Something clearly was *not* right! From fifteen feet away, I saw long, brown hair and a cute, petite young woman. As I stood in front of Tanya DeVoe I was absolutely shocked! It didn't take me more than two seconds to make the determination that this was not the Tanya I had met and teased at the school on October 22, 1997. This was not the Tanya to whom I had given a book.

The person I was viewing had brown, curled hair lying gently on her shoulders. Her petite body was dressed in a stunning silver formal gown with matching gloves, her prom dress. A grieving young man I met a few moments later would attest to the fact that he wouldn't have a date for prom that year.

Everything in me wanted to run from the scene. Instead, I turned to my right and extended my hand to the grieving mother.

"Kathy, I am so sorry for your loss," was all I could muster.

"What's your name?" she asked.

"My name is Steve. I am an author who spoke to the kids at the school last October," I said. Kathy's face lit ever so little.

"Oh, you're the one who sent Tanya the card," she whispered. "That meant a lot to her. In fact, I'm pretty sure it's still on her dresser," she stated. I really didn't know what to say in my confusion, but I did the best I could.

"I'm so glad it blessed her. Obviously, your daughter was a very special young lady and her life impacted many people. God bless you," I said and hugged the grieving woman.

I shook hands with her grieving husband, Rick, and then promptly made a beeline for the door. I said goodbye to Jackie and left. It was a challenging ride home.

I waited a few weeks before I made a call that was burning inside me like an inferno. I picked up the phone and dialed.

"Jackie, it wasn't appropriate to talk to you the night of the wake, but I have a question for you now."

"Okay," she said rather softly.

"Do you remember when I asked you for the address of the Tanya in your class? The one to whom I had given a book last October and then followed up with a note?"

"Yeah, of course. Tanya talked about that note a lot, Steve. I mentioned that the day I called to tell you she died."

"Yes, I remember. I'm grateful it meant something to her," I said before getting to the heart of my call. "Well, Jackie, you're not going to believe what I'm going to tell you. You see, I'm 99% sure that the young woman I saw in that casket on April 2nd was not the same one I met at your school in October."

There was total silence on the other end.

"The girl I met that day in your classroom was blonde, wore glasses, and had an entirely different physique than the girl I saw at Newcomer Funeral Home."

More silence. It felt like an eternity, but it was only seconds from the revelation I would receive of the mystery that had left me baffled for the last few weeks.

"Oh, my God!" Jackie gasped under her breath. "There are a couple of Tanyas at our school. When you called in January looking for "Tanya" I thought you meant Tanya DeVoe, so I gave you her address. From your description, clearly you are describing Tanya Dundee. I'm sorry, I gave you the address of the wrong girl!"*

The Story of the Story

Okay, so the letter went to the "wrong" girl, which may have been the "right" girl after all. Here's why.

On April 5, 1998, three days after Tanya DeVoe's wake, I was speaking in a small church. After the service, the man who had hosted me for the weekend was absolutely adamant that I meet one of the people from the congregation. He said she was a very special woman. When I asked him why he thought this was necessary, he said, "Because, she's an author, too."

About an hour after the service, we were getting into our car to go to meet her when unbelievably she pulled into the church parking lot! She never told us why she came back to the church. Soon, she had handed me a book on grief that she had written in 1996. She had lost her 20-year-old son and daughter-in-law in a motorcycle accident. The book chronicled the debilitating grieving process she went through and how she came out stronger on the other side. I told her that I had attended Tanya DeVoe's wake just days before, and how difficult it was to see the pain in her parents' eyes.

Having never been through the grieving process myself, the book opened my eyes to what people go through during this experience. I was so impressed with the book that I sent a copy of it to Kathy and Rick DeVoe a few months later. When I phoned Kathy DeVoe she told me that she was grateful that I had sent it, that although she was still deeply grieving over Tanya, the book was of great help and comfort to her.

It was then, and only then, that I began to see just why the card to Tanya sent in January may have gotten to not only the "right" girl, but also the "right" family. You see, the woman who I met in that parking lot that day in 1998 was the mother of the "Baby on the Blanket," who because of God's mercy had watched her life and that of her child spared in 1975! Could it possibly be that God had this in mind when I sent that card? It certainly is something to think about.

By the way, the mother of the "Baby on the Blanket" is now my wife!

The Policeman Who Went to Church

It was going to be an ordinary Sunday evening service at the Spokane Family Worship Center in Seattle. However, there would be a special speaker, a policeman, who was going to give a testimony about how he was able to use his job as a witness for God.

Jo was visiting the church while attending a conference. The year is 1985. Sitting to her left was Mrs. Treats, the wife of Pastor Casey Treats. On the right of Jo was another young woman, Jean, who was a part of a ministry called Teen Challenge. After worship, announcements, and taking an offering, the policeman was asked to come to the podium to share how he reconciles the challenges of being an officer and a Christian.

"Thank you for being here tonight," he began. "I'd be lying to you if I told you that it was easy being an officer and a Christian," he confessed.

He acknowledged that in his line of work he had to put up with all kinds of "interesting" people, from speeders and belligerent drunks on the highway to the druggies and prostitutes on the streets.

"It challenges you," he mentioned.

The whole while he spoke, Jo noticed Jean beginning to fidget. She seemed somewhat uneasy.

"Was she in trouble?" Jo wondered.

A while later, the officer opened up the service to questions from the congregation. He answered everything from what it's like to be shot at to what he enjoyed most about his job. Someone then posed an interesting question.

"What's it like to try to arrest a drunk man?"

"You know," the officer began with a little smirk. "Actually, women are worse than men."

"Really?" said the questioner.

"Oh, yeah. As a matter of fact, about a year ago, I had to arrest a woman for prostitution. She was extremely drunk. When I went to put the handcuffs on her she went berserk!" said the policeman.

Jo noticed Jean was beginning to become emotional. She must have been connecting in some way with the officer's remarks. Then the man continued.

"I mean to tell you this woman was downright mean. She yelled and she screamed, she kicked, clawed and scratched me for a couple minutes until we got her under control," he recalled.

Jo looked at Jean again. Now she was crying heavily into Kleenex pressed against her face. She let out a loud whimper and then could not contain herself any longer. She bolted out of her seat and ran down the aisle toward the officer.

"It was me! It was me!" she wailed as she ran the length of the aisle to the front of the sanctuary. She literally threw herself into arms of the officer. "It was me who you were trying to arrest that day," she sobbed. "I'm so sorry. I've been praying that God would help me find you so that I could tell you I'm sorry!"

The Story of the Story

An indescribable hush came over the church during this divine appointment and answer to a former hellion's prayer. It was brought to our attention that there was quite some distance between the church where this tearful reunion took place, and where the actual arrest had happened. We don't feel the story would be tarnished or any less of a "Godincidence" if both events had taken place in the city of Seattle, but it certainly makes it more intriguing when you realize the likelihood of the reunion taking place given they were from different areas.

Through the very experience of hitting the bottom, Jean had had a radical conversion and had come to faith in the Lord in her jail cell. Her childlike prayer to meet the policeman again who had arrested her to say she was sorry was answered through a "Godincidence."

Fishing by Light

Dale Van Elsen was passionate about fishing. That's what he and his friends were off to do in Canada in May of 1997. This was an annual event for Dan and Dave Doering, Tom Brantmeier, Jim Brown and Ron Jacobi, but it was Dale's maiden voyage. Without question it would be one he would remember for the rest of his life. They made the 11-hour drive in two trucks each pulling a boat.

After unpacking clothes, food and gear, the fishermen made their way to the boats they had moored on White Lake, in the Canadian Province of Ontario. Everyone was looking forward to a week of relaxation, fun, and their sport. It was a rainy, cold, overcast day. At times the rain turned into puffy snowflakes. Because of the frigid conditions the fishermen dressed in snowmobile suits, heavy boots and raingear over the top of their clothing in an attempt to stay warm and dry.

The two boats floating about thirty feet apart from each other each held three men. The fishing expedition was well under way, but was relatively uneventful. In an attempt to remove snow from his boots before it could melt, Dale, who was up front, stood up. At precisely the same time, another one of the men sitting in the back stood up. In a split second there was a splash. Dale had fallen overboard! Because the front is shallower where Dale was, when he stood up and then the man in the back stood up, Dale was immediately thrown off balance.

"Oh, my God," yelled one of the men.

Pandemonium hit the waves. The men felt absolutely helpless as they stared at the swirling water that had swallowed their friend and fishing buddy. The men in the other boat heard the commotion, but assumed that the crew was trying to net a "big one." Deep below the surface of the ice-cold Canadian water, Dale's mind raced trying to determine what to do. In the midst of his panic an overwhelming sense of calm came over him. The heavy water-soaked clothing was pulling him deeper into the water, a potentially fatal problem.

"The first thing I need to do is get out of these boots," he thought. His boots had already filled with freezing water. He reached down to try to pull them off, but with no success. His clothing was dragging him deeper and deeper by the moment. Surrounded by eerie, pitch-black darkness, another challenge came to his mind. He realized he couldn't tell if he was upside down or right side up in the water.

"Which way is it to the surface?" he wondered, as his heart lodged in his throat.

Dale did the only thing he knew to do in that lonely and frightening moment and that was to pray. He felt himself tiring and his entire body seemingly got heavier and heavier during his fight for life.

"Dear God, help me! There's no way I'm going to be able to do this on my own," he confessed.

Dale looked around in the murky blackness of the ice-cold water for the boat's anchor and saw the rope to which it was attached. Suddenly he looked up and saw a bright light! Although he had been in the water for only a few short seconds he was almost out of breath. Without another thought, he swam ferociously toward the light, knowing that time was slipping away. In about seven seconds, after swimming upward about eight feet, he arrived at the surface. To his relief, both boats were there. It was going to be a struggle to pull Dales 6'3" 220-pound frame into the boat.

When Dale came to the surface and realized where he was, he grabbed on to the front of the boat. Dave tried to get Dale into the boat, but couldn't pull him in, so he yelled for Dan to bring the second boat over to help. With Dan lifting from behind and Dave pulling from the front they were able to get Dale in the boat.

"C'mon, buddy, we gotcha!" said Dan Doering pulling Dale into the safety of the boat.

Disaster had been averted and no one was praying or counting his blessings more than Dale Van Elsen. The men were afraid that because of the snow and cold Dale would develop hypothermia before they could get him the twelve miles back to the shore. Then there was a three-mile trip back to the campsite itself, but at least they would have some heat in the vehicle. There was little conversation on the way back to shore or to the campsite.

Later, sitting around the fire in warm, dry clothes, Dale appeared to be doing well. Clearly the unspoken desire of every man's heart was that he would fully recover from the trauma. Dale expressed his deep gratitude to each of the men for their help, but one thing in particular was on his mind.

"Man, thanks you guys for shining the flashlight into the water," he began. "I had no clue where I was or which way was up. If you guys hadn't done that, well, I'd be dead," he said in the hush of the moment.

The men looked with confusion at one another and then at Dale.

"Dale, we don't know what you're talking about. Nobody shined any flashlight into the water!"

The Nightgown Story

Connie Campbell was a single parent, dealing with all the challenges that come with single parenting. It was 1986. Connie owned a house, but by the time she paid the mortgage and bought food, there was seldom enough left to pay the heating bill. So, she kept the thermostat well below the comfort level. Working three jobs was the routine of her life. She and her son, Barry, 18, worked hard to make ends meet. They fixed up the house as much as they could afford to. It was livable, but there were certainly no amenities. In fact, it took almost fifty pounds of cement to level the kitchen floor enough to put a table and chairs on it.

Concerned for Connie and Barry, Connie's dad installed a space heater in their home. It required that whatever room was being heated be blocked off in order that that room would hold the heat. By evening, it not only got cold outside, but it got cold in the house, too. Connie vividly recalls waking on some winter mornings, going into the shower and seeing her breath! Needless to say, Connie wore a long, flannel night-gown for warmth, but the nightgown Connie was wearing at the time had been given to her by her grandmother and had worn quite thin.

A few days after Christmas, Connie went to Target and found a Christmas ornament for 25 cents. As she headed to the checkout counter, she walked past the flannel nightgowns that were on sale. Even discounted, it was still not within her means to purchase one. It didn't stop her, however, from praying to God for a nightgown, just like the one she had seen on the shelf at Target.

"God, I need a new flannel nightgown so badly. You know the one I'm wearing has worn pretty thin," she prayed. "I don't care if You have someone give one to me or if You help me find one at a rummage sale. I'll be grateful for it, no matter how You provide it for me."

Connie paid for her ornament and walked out of the store, forgetting about the request. The very next day Connie prepared to go to church. It was a chilly Sunday. For some reason, she decided to take a different route than usual. It had snowed one-to-two slushy inches of sloppy, wet snow that made for messy driving. As she turned into a residential neighborhood, Connie noticed something in the middle of the street. Always one to love a surprise, she never missed an opportunity to check out anything laying in the road.

Connie pulled over to the curb of the street in the highly populated area and got out of her car. She took a look around, somewhat cautious and embarrassed, as she approached the article in the middle of the street.

At first glance Connie noticed a pair of slippers peaking out of the plastic bag. Then she noticed an article of clothing with tags still attached to it hanging out of the bag also. She scooped the entire package out of the wet slush.

As she pulled it toward her, her heart nearly burst through her chest as she realized what she was holding. It was a white, flannel nightgown with pink flowers, and it was exactly her size!

The Story of the Story

Connie put the gown on the floor of her car. It was wet. She didn't care. She began to cry. It was a pivotal moment in her life and faith. In that moment, Connie had a peace in her heart that God would be there to take care of her and her son. He has.

Today, Connie Campbell is a very successful businesswoman. Her office building has plenty of heat. And, oh, Connie wants you to know that God shops at K-Mart!

A Love that Knows No Bounds

It was a hot and muggy Saturday morning, June 20, 1998. A crowd had gathered at Appleton Alliance church for a funeral to honor a wonderful man of integrity, Don Grady. Don had pre-planned the service. He did not want the focus of the service to be about him, but rather God's plan of salvation and the reason for hope beyond the grave.

Following singing of "Old Rugged Cross" and a prayer, Neil Zuberbier made his way to the pulpit to eulogize a man he considered to be not just a friend, but also his spiritual father. Although Neil would try to find words that would adequately describe his feelings for Don, he felt nothing he could say would be enough to pay his respects properly. As honored as he was to have been chosen to speak on behalf of the family, Neil knew what he was about to do was going to be difficult, perhaps the most emotionally demanding experience of his life.

Don Grady had been diagnosed with cancer in 1997. Neil Zuberbier's relationship with Don and his wife, Carol, had grown even closer during this challenging time. This triangular relationship had begun back in the '80s, but after nearly a ten-year lapse, it had resurfaced again when Neil returned "home" in 1992 after living out west. Years of living in rebellion had cost Neil dearly. He suffered the consequences of his many poor choices, including spending three years in prison. All the while, Don and Carol Grady were praying for Neil.

The Gradys and many others knew Neil was not new to trouble. They began praying for him shortly after they met him in the mid '80s. News that Neil had been incarcerated in a South Dakota Correctional Facility in 1989 came as no surprise to the Gradys. Years prior, the Gradys had put their reputations on the line, more than once, when they'd arrive in court to ask judges to be lenient with Neil. Their actions toward Neil displayed that they loved him almost as much as they did their own children.

Shortly after Don and Carol Grady met Neil Zuberbier, they faithfully began to pray for him to come to his senses, to "shape up" and, better yet, to turn his life over to God. In 1989, that's exactly what happened. A once suicidal Neil had written the Gradys to inform them that after years of hell raising, disobedience and legal troubles, he got down on his knees in a jail cell in South Dakota and asked Jesus to be his Savior. The Gradys were thrilled. God had answered their prayers.

Neil recalls with fondness the day he unexpectedly and quite miraculously came face-to-face with Don and Carol only a few years after writing to them about his conversion.

"I had just been released from a prison in South Dakota in1992. When I returned to Appleton I made the decision to go to a Sunday morning service at First Assembly of God. I couldn't believe it!" he said. "I saw Don and Carol. I made my way over to them. I was so excited. I hugged both of them tightly and thanked them for their prayers," he recalled. "I could see the joy in their eyes that I had asked God into my life."

Within 60 days of that wonderful Sunday reunion, the Gradys and Neil were headed to Florida on a missions trip. Neil was at the wheel for a good share of the 31-hour trip. In spite of the fact that the Gradys knew of Neil's "shaky" driving record and his propensity to have a "lead foot," Don and Carol had no worries. They all made it to Florida and back fine. Neil knew that what he was experiencing with the Gradys was special and unique. You see, Neil knew first hand that the Gradys had gone through a "hell" of their own.

The Gradys could have become hardened people and could have rebelled against God after having experienced the suffering they had. The biggest trial occurred just fifteen years before Don's death.

It was a pleasant Tuesday in 1983. The Grady's son, Bill, 16, had an appointment in Madison at the University Hospital for a checkup. The drive would take about two hours, so the day began early at the Grady's household. Beth, 12, wanted to stay home, but Carol insisted that she come along with Don, Carol and Bill. She was simply too young to remain at home alone and unattended. So the four got into the Grady car and off they went. Don drove. Carol was seated in the passenger seat.

Beth sat directly behind her Dad so Bill sat behind Carol, a switch for the two children.

The Gradys had barely gone five miles when they came to a curve that bent to the left. Immediately Don could see that tragedy was looming ahead. A car was coming at them! The blue 1976 Camaro was unable to negotiate the curve, crossed the centerline, and rammed into their car just in front of Don's door.

Although it felt like an eternity to the Gradys, it was only a short time before paramedics were on the scene. Don, Carol and Bill were not seriously injured. However, in the back seat, young Beth would not be as fortunate. She had been killed instantly. A drunk 21-year-old with glazed eyes, who had "come to" from behind the steering wheel of his own smashed vehicle, was wandering the scene in utter shock and incoherence. He stumbled over to the Grady vehicle and saw Beth dead in the back seat. All he could hear was Carol's voice echoing in his ears, "Where's my baby?"

Over 100 stitches would be needed to close the multiple lacerations Don had incurred. He had also suffered major chest injuries. Carol had suffered head and neck injuries. In time they would come to learn more about the man who had robbed them of their precious Beth. He was basically a good kid who had been partying into the early morning hours before the accident.

It wasn't long into the grieving process that the Holy Spirit of God began to deal with the Gradys urging them to forgive this young man. One would understand why this would not have been easy for them, if even possible at all.

Still, Don and Carol chose to do what they felt was right. They sent a letter to the young man's parents.

"We know you are suffering as much as we are. Please tell your son we have forgiven him and we're praying for him."

To this day, the Grady family will tell anyone who'll listen that God can bring something good out of tragedy. They will also tell you that the loss of their daughter was one of the most difficult experiences of their lives, but that God used it to draw them even closer to Him and each other as He comforted them. Neil Zuberbier's story is another proof that

God *can* bring forth good from bad and even tragic situations.

So, as Neil Zuberbier stood in the pulpit sharing at Don's funeral just how much he loved this man, his tears flowed freely and unashamedly. Neil will tell you that he really isn't a public speaker at all, but on this day one would have never known. A calm had settled over him and each word he spoke was a glowing tribute to someone he loved with all his heart, Don Grady.

Judging from the response of those in attendance the family had made a great choice of a person to pay tribute to Don. Neil shared a few of the more special memories he had of Don including the fact that Don had been the "stand in" father who had escorted his bride, Rheta, down the aisle to marry him in 1994. As he closed his tribute, Neil looked at the gray casket in front of him. How grateful he felt to have known such a remarkable man.

A reasonably good case could be made that the Gradys are a bit unique and unusual. Their actions over the years had proven that they could love "the unlovable" and forgive "the unforgivable." Given that alone, they were an extraordinary family for sure. We told you that Don and Carol Grady had met Neil Zuberbier in the 1980s. Specifically, it was August 9, 1983 when they "ran into each other" quite literally.

You see, the 21-year-old drunk who recklessly smashed into the Gradys in 1983, killing their 12-year-old daughter Beth, was none other than Neil Zuberbier himself!

The Story of the Story

Now that you've read the ending, we'd like to suggest you read the story again. First of all, its message is quite profound and perhaps you'll learn something new the second time through. Second, you'll notice we tried to put a few subtleties in the story that wouldn't have made any sense when you first read it. Did you catch the fact that the Gradys rode with Neil for 31 hours to Florida in 1993? Do you think that took some faith?

Steve was blessed to have been at Don Grady's funeral. He had met Don and Carol only two years earlier in church. He had known Neil since 1993. It was Neil who made Steve aware of this remarkable story.

An Egg and a Zucchini

Things were not going well for the Palomares. Julie and Alex had been married a little more than a year and were living in Puebla, Mexico. It was February of 1982. Julie was a student at the University of Americas. Alex was unemployed, a situation that did not appear to be changing anytime soon. As can be the case where there is no job, there is little money, and consequently little food.

The young couple in their early twenties had not told anyone of their problems. They were very much out of touch with the world in general, and the people around them for the most part, with the exception of their church family. They had no telephone or form of transportation. The trip to church required two stops on the bus.

Alex grew up in Mexico the second oldest of eleven children, so hard times were nothing new to him. Julie, however, grew up in the United States where her basic needs had always been met. Even during this difficult time, Alex suggested to his wife they be grateful.

It was about 1 o'clock in the afternoon when Alex asked his wife a pointed question.

"Julie, what do we have in the refrigerator?"

"Just a zucchini and an egg," she replied.

"Go ahead and make it."

"What do you mean, make it?" asked his wife.

"Go ahead and cook it," he insisted.

"What in the world can we make with only a zucchini and an egg?" she asked.

"Go ahead and cook them," he reiterated.

Julie proceeded to slice the zucchini. She scrambled the egg and added the zucchini to the pan. Before they ate Alex had a question for his wife.

"Have you ever had a hungry day in your life?"

"Never," said Julie.

"Well, I've had many of them," said Alex. "Honey, let's pray."

With words of gratitude from Alex's mouth to God's ear, they ate. They no sooner had finished and got up from the table when there was a knock. Julie went to the door. Standing there were two familiar faces, elders from their church.

They had brought two gifts for the Palomares. One elder handed the couple the first gift, an envelope with 1500 pesos, equivalent to $75 to $100. The second gift came in the form of a stranger's business card handed to Alex by the other elder.

"Alex," he said, "the man whose name is on this card would like to interview you and give you a job!"

The Story of the Story

What the Palamares couldn't have known was that at the exact time that they were praying, the elders, who were out doing visitation to counsel and encourage the church family, felt compelled to make a visit to Julie and Alex. Julie and Alex can attest that God is "seldom early and never late."

Snow Time to Worry

Stacy Thompson was feeling uneasy, even somewhat worried, about the holiday trip on which she and her husband, Bob, were going to be embarking.

"Bob, I don't want to go," said Stacy, unable to really communicate to him why. After all, from Menominee to Escanaba was only a 60-minute trip, and weather forecasts, even for the Upper Peninsula, were looking promising. Still, she was not happy about the trip.

However, Bob was excited about the thought of seeing his family and friends "back home."

"Aw, c'mon, honey, it'll be fun," he told his wife.

Stacy agreed to go with her husband. On the trip north she had a small, eerie voice telling her to be prepared for something. Stacy knew their big four-wheel drive Ford pickup was as reliable a vehicle as any, but Stacy still felt unsafe, which was unlike her.

Stacy prayed for God's safety for their trip, but also found herself making mental notes about what to do if the truck went off the road and rolled over. She could not bring herself to share with Bob the fear that she was feeling during the trip, and actually had begun to feel even before they had left home.

The trip turned out to be uneventful and Bob and Stacy arrived safely in Escanaba. Christmas of 1980 turned out to be a wonderful celebration with family and friends as planned. Bob and Stacy had been married only a year earlier in California, so this was their first "white Christmas" up north. All too soon it was time for the couple to say their goodbyes. It was dusk as the Thompsons headed back south for home.

Barely into the trip, the skies darkened and it started to snow. As they continued on, Stacy began to feel quite nervous. Snow blew across the road and whirled around in the wind and the temperatures dropped below freezing. Driving conditions were quickly deteriorating, but Bob was a good driver and that did bring Stacy some peace. Still, she prayed and found herself mentally wondering, once again, what she would do if something happened. She would roll to the floor and brace herself. For now, the truck was toasty and soothing Christmas music filled the cab as Bob navigated toward home.

Stacy began to relax once she realized they were now only twenty minutes from home. She laid her head softly on Bob's lap and soon she was fast asleep, but not for long. Suddenly she awoke to hear Bob's voice in a panic.

"Hang on, we're sliding!" he said.

Stacy realized there was no time to buckle her seatbelt. She knew what to do. She rolled to the floor and braced herself, just like she had mentally rehearsed. What seemed like hours took actually only seconds and the details are still recorded in vivid detail in her mind to this day. Their truck slid into the oncoming lane, across the gravel shoulder of the highway and then careened onward, hitting a downed tree and flipping end-over-end. Stacy was bouncing around the cab when one question flooded her mind.

"What if I die?"

Instantly she heard a voice speak clearly, but calmly, to her. "No matter what happens, you'll be fine."

Immediately a peace settled over her, and then she passed out. Some time later, Stacy awoke, dazed and slightly confused as she felt herself being cradled in a strong man's arms and carried away from the truck. She was laid ever so gently on her back in the snow. Stunned and unable to speak, it brought a sense of peace and assurance to know that Bob was unharmed.

Finally, fully aware of her surroundings, Stacy looked around but couldn't see Bob anywhere.

"Where did he go?" she wondered.

Again, she remembered the words, "No matter what happens, you'll be fine."

"Bob, where are you?" Stacy called out in barely a whisper.

Her lungs were so compressed that she could hardly breathe, but the peace she had experienced earlier was still with her. Then, in the stillness of the night, she heard the sound of holiday music coming from the cab of the truck. Stacy glanced across her left shoulder to see that the truck had landed upright on its wheels. Again, she couldn't help but wonder, "Where is Bob?"

Suddenly a muffled voice came from deep inside the vehicle.

"Stacy, are you all right?"

It was Bob! Oh, what joy it brought Stacy to know that, just as the voice had told her, they would be fine.

Both Bob and Stacy were taken to the hospital where they were treated and released. The Thompsons had survived what could have been a deadly tragedy. Stacy is grateful for what she knows were words of the Lord's warning and comfort to her during that trip. But, to this day, there is also a mystery that Stacy has never been able to dismiss that still begs a question, and it's a good one.

"If Bob was trapped in the cab that cold, snowy night, then who was the man who carried her from the truck and laid her in the snow?"

Even the Winds and the Sea Obey Him

In the early days of the Calvary Chapel Ministries, Pastor Dwight was a part of the communal ministry. It was set up in such a way as to provide opportunities for the young people to attend Bible School. To that end, some of them would work to provide the financial means for others to go to school. Then the graduates would work so the others could attend. One of the positions included working various jobs at the Minneapolis Airport. Dwight had become discouraged with his tasks at the airport.

"God, I want to quit. I don't want to do this anymore," he prayed as he was mopping the terminal floor.

God was concerned about Dwight, so concerned that He knew what was best for him. Apparently He had other ideas of what was in Dwight's best interest at this juncture of his life.

As the 25-year old cleaned the large airport, he came upon a Billy Graham Evangelistic poster on a wall. The big letters read, "Even the winds and the sea obey Him." The young Christian felt in his heart that God was speaking to him, directing him to be patient, grateful, and obedient. He interpreted this to mean that he was to continue to be a janitor.

"Okay, Lord, I get it. Even nature obeys you; I should too," he humbly acquiesced. So with the literal sign on the wall and a "sign" from God, he continued in his janitorial duties.

A year later, in 1977, Dwight himself went to Bible School. He was ordained as a pastor in '78 and went on to start his own church. He has been pastoring it ever since. One of the true delights and privileges of his position has been to take tour groups from the church to Israel. Every other year he has been doing so since 1979.

In 2001, preparations were being made for another trip to the Holy Land. The size of the group would range from 50 to 60 people. The group's travel itinerary was generally from Appleton or Green Bay to Chicago to Tel Aviv, a total of about ten hours in flight. The length of the tour would be two weeks. The travel itself was uneventful as they arrived in Israel safely once more.

Meanwhile, two-thousand-miles to the west of Appleton in southern California, a woman was making the five thousand mile flight to Israel. It would be her responsibility to see that Pastor's tour group from Calvary not only had a wonderful time, but to help everything go as smoothly as possible.

One day the crew from Calvary and another woman boarded a forty-foot tour boat. It was common for Pastor Dwight to base his Bible teachings on whatever area they found themselves in on that day. Well, on this particular day, as they sailed on the peaceful water, Dwight caught himself smiling knowing he had a story to tell that would tie in beautifully with their current location on the Sea of Galilee.

"I want to share a story with you from 25 years ago that I feel is very appropriate for today's teaching. It's based on a passage out of the book of Matthew," he began. "I was a young man, assigned to be a janitor in the Minneapolis-St. Paul Airport. I was tired of it and wanted to quit."

He then told of encountering the Billy Graham poster and how it reminded him "Even the winds and the sea obey Him." He shared that God had used this to capture his attention to the fact that God is always looking further down the road than we are. He acknowledged to the group how grateful he was that God had His way. Dwight humbly suggested that just possibly, if he had left that job without God's approval, he might not have been on this boat today.

No sooner had he finished his message than a woman approached him, insisting that she speak with him.

"Pastor, my name is Joyce. I work for *Inspired Travel* out of California. I was listening to your story very closely when I realized your name was familiar. I so much appreciated your message, but what I wanted to tell you, which you may not remember, is that I was your boss at the Minneapolis Airport in 1976!"

The Story of the Story

As Steve sat with Dwight to listen to this story, it became quite clear to him that Dwight felt that meeting Joyce was his confirmation that he had done the right thing by not quitting that job when he clearly wanted "out."

Colorado Christmas

A crisp, clean snow was falling on Christmas Eve of 1991 over Colorado Springs, Colorado. Meet Tammy and Steve Lenert, newlyweds with a blended family of seven children. It fell to Steve to bear the responsibility of addressing the children concerning what would be happening or, better put, what wouldn't. Steve and Tammy both had low paying jobs; Tammy was a receptionist and Steve worked in a hardware store. With only $10 between them, there would be no gifts under the tree this year.

They all gathered in the living room, Chris 13, Justin 11, Nick 7, Brittany 3, Jessica 5, Anthony 5, and Little Chris, 3. Tammy sat next to Steve as he spoke to the family.

"Kids, your mom and I want to tell you how very much we love you. We want to remind you of the real reason for Christmas, that Jesus was born so that He would go to the cross and die to pay for our sins," he said. "We would love to be able to give you all gifts, but this year we just can't," Steve went on to say.

Although the kids understood, clearly they were not thrilled with the news.

Steve no sooner got the words out of his mouth than the family could hear Christmas carolers singing. The family got up and went to the picture window. Standing out on the sidewalk in front of their house were thirty young men and women holding bags bearing gifts. They were from the Lenert's church.

"Hark the herald angels sing, glory to the newborn King," they sang.

The Lenerts were deeply touched by every word that had originally come from the mouths of the angels. After the singers got through serenading the family with God's love, they came to the door. Out of the bags came a beautifully wrapped and tagged gift for each child in the family! At the bottom of one bag were two more gifts; one was for Steve and one for Tammy. Steve and Tammy looked at the scene and began to weep.

The family expressed their gratitude for the outpouring of Christmas cheer that would make this holiday season one to remember.

The next morning Steve called the pastor to express his appreciation for what the church had done for the family. He planned to be brief knowing the pastor was celebrating the birth of Christ with his own family.

"Pastor, it's Steve Lenert. Merry Christmas."

"And a Merry Christmas to you, too," pastor said joyfully.

"I won't keep you long," assured Steve. "Thanks so much for the gifts for our family," he said gratefully. "Man, if you could have seen the faces of the kids!" he reported with his voice trailing off a bit due to the unexpected lump in his throat.

"Aw, we knew that it would bless you and we were glad to do it. The carolers said that the looks on the faces of your kids were priceless," he finished. "Have a great day."

Steve had one more quick thought to add before letting the pastor go.

"Oh, by the way, I also wanted to say thanks for the necklace for Tammy and the money clip for me, too," said Steve.

"Huh?" questioned pastor, who clearly had no clue what Steve was talking about.

"Yeah, we also want to thank you for including the gifts for Tammy and me."

There was silence on the other end of the line before the pastor replied.

"Uh, I don't know what you're talking about," said the pastor. "We went shopping just for gifts for the kids. Steve, there weren't any gifts in those bags for you or Tammy!"

The Story of the Story

Steve Lenert's face gleamed as he recalled the "Colorado Christmas Eve Miracle." To this day, the story remains that the church only shopped for gifts for the Lenert children. After purchasing them, they returned to the church and wrapped them.

The pastor has always rigorously denied ever buying or including any gifts for Steve and Tammy in the bags of the carolers that night. Steve still smiles at the irony of God giving him a money clip, especially on that particular Christmas.

Today, the Lenert family members are all doing fine. When they need a jolt of gratitude, they simply remind themselves of a Christmas Eve from years past.

The Night the TV Talked

Don Koepke was a fast walker and a fast talker. He loved living in the "fast" lane, but the thing he most loved to do was drink. Don was a businessman. Part of his job required him to be out and about with other businessmen. This meant that he had a ready excuse to drink. His wife, Marion, his family and friends could see that Don had a problem with alcohol, but he was a master at justifying his actions and denying his problem. An intervention would be coming, but not in the ordinary fashion.

After a hard night of drinking, Don came home to do what he normally did. He cracked open a beer and plopped down in his La-Z-boy to watch a little late-night TV. Marion was already sound asleep. Don clicked through several stations until he landed at *The 700 Club*, a popular Christian program.

Pat Robertson, one of the hosts of the program, was telling the TV audience that coming up would be an interview with an alcoholic after the show went to a break. Don put his feet up and lit a cigarette. What he saw next made him wonder if he had wandered into the *"Twilight Zone."* Sitting on the right side of *The 700 Club* set was co-host Ben Kinchlow. On the other side of the set, being interviewed, was indeed an alcoholic. It was Don himself!

Don felt like he had been slapped in the face by the ice-cold hand of reality as he watched himself being interviewed. It didn't take long for Don to get the message. He was an alcoholic who needed help. On the bottom of the TV screen was a toll-free number that viewers could call to ask for help and prayer. He jotted down the number on a scrap piece of paper next to the empty beer can and headed to his office at the end of the hallway. It was 3 a.m. CST as he sat down at his desk and dialed the number. After only two rings a woman answered.

"Hello, *The 700 Club*. This is Kathy."

"Hi, my name is Don. I was just watching your program and saw Ben interviewing an alcoholic," he said. "I think that's me. I need help," he confessed.

At this point Don did not dare to mention to Kathy that the man he saw being interviewed was himself. She offered to pray for him and he accepted. Kathy assured him that God could help him to "beat the bottle," but he would have to do his part and choose not to drink once he hung up.

"Is there anything else I can do to help you?" asked Kathy.

"No, you've been a big help already," replied Don and hung up.

Don went right to bed and slept better that night than he had in a long time.

The following morning he told Marion that he had called *The 700 Club*. He admitted that he was an alcoholic. Marion was relieved to know that her prayers were on the verge of being answered. Don, however, wasn't quite through with having a "taste of liquor" from time to time. He continued to frequent the martini lounges just long enough to realize that he simply could not maintain this lifestyle any longer.

On June 7, 1982, Don Koepke made a life-changing decision to enter a treatment facility for alcoholism. One day at a time, with God's grace, Don beat the addiction, just as Kathy and God had promised he would.

Months later, in the fall, Don and Marion received a phone call from Marion's sister, Margo, in Virginia Beach, Virginia. She and her husband, Jim, asked Don and Marion to come out to visit them. Margo had a great idea for something to do once they arrived.

"Marion, I'll try to get tickets for *The 700 Club* while you're here," she said.

The 700 Club is based in Virginia Beach. Because of its popularity and a limited number of tickets per show, there was some question as to the possibility of attaining tickets for a specific date. Not only did Margo get tickets, but they were for the front row!

Don and Marion flew to Virginia in late November. Their tickets for the live broadcast of *The 700 Club* were dated for November 29. They arrived early and were escorted to their seats along with approximately two hundred others in the audience. One of the producers was passing out pieces of white paper to each of the audience members.

"Ladies and gentlemen," said one of the producers. "One of the things we like to do is take questions from our studio audience. If you have one, please write it down on the paper we have given you and someone will be by shortly to pick it up."

He went on to further explain the process.

"If we pick your question, we will bring it back to you before the start of the show for the question and answer part of the program, all right? Any questions?"

There weren't any.

Many audience participants jotted down their questions. Another producer gathered the slips of paper and took them back to the set. Minutes later one of the producers approached Margo. Her question had been selected. Soon theme music was rolling and the voice introduced the program.

"Welcome to *The 700 Club*. Here is your host, Pat Robertson!"

After the first segment, they took a commercial break. At the break, Ben Kinchlow grabbed his microphone and made his way down toward Margo. She was going to be invited to be the first one to ask a question after the break, but before he could even reach Margo, Don (recalling the "interview" back in May) had something he wanted to say to Ben.

"Ben, I'd like to talk with you after the show. I've got a great story for you."

"Really? What's up, man?" he tried to ask, only to realize they were coming back out of a commercial.

"Welcome back to *The 700 Club*," said Pat Robertson. "It's time for questions from our audience. Here's Ben."

"Thanks, Pat. Before we get to our questions, I had a brother here tell me he had a story to share. Hello, what's your name and what do you have for us?" he said, totally surprising Don.

Don, seldom lost for words, felt blindsided by the surprise.

"Uh, I was watching your show back in May and I saw you interview an alcoholic. It was then that I knew I had a problem, so I called and talked with one of your counselors. Shortly after that, I went and got help. Thanks to you and *The 700 Club*, and the power of prayer, I've been sober ever since!"

"Halleluiah!" said Ben as the crowd cheered in appreciation of Don's testimony.

A still-stunned Don sat down. He purposely had left out the same detail that he'd also not told Kathy back in May, which was that the alcoholic he had seen Ben interviewing was himself!

After an hour, the show was over. No sooner had the set gone dark than a young woman came rushing down the stairs from a booth right above the studio audience seating. She made her way toward the Koepkes and the Koehnkes.

"Hi there!" she said. "Don, I'm Kathy, the one who took your call in May!" she said delightedly.

"Well, nice to meet you," said Don as he extended a handshake to "the voice" on the other end of that special call.

"I remember it very well," she recalled. "It was four o'clock in the morning, right?"

"That's right," confirmed Don.

That fact was correct. Don called at about 3 a.m. CST, making it 4 a.m. EST in Virginia Beach.

"I'm so glad you're doing well, Don. What a joy to have met!" she said as she headed back toward the booth.

Months passed. Don and Marion's marriage continued to get stronger. Don continued to get healthier physically, emotionally and spiritually. In May of 1983 the phone rang. It was *The 700 Club* asking if they could come to the Koepke's home to do a story about Don and his decision for sobriety through God's help and *The 700 Club*."

Both Don and Marion agreed to allow their story to be told.

Nearly a year after Don's call for help, the TV crew spent a few days and tons of footage filming interviews and reenactments of Don's life as a drunk turned believer.

The crew returned to Virginia Beach to edit the tape. Then the phone rang at the Koepke's again. In reviewing the tape, the crew had discovered something very baffling. They told Don that they could not find the tape of the interview Don said he had seen the year before. Although *The 700 Club* checked all the tapes done during May, and two months prior, no program interviewing an alcoholic could be found.

Now Don himself was baffled, so he decided to do some checking of his own. He knew that the Green Bay TV affiliate that ran *The 700 Club* was WLRE, TV-26. He also knew the affiliate's owner, Jerry Newman. Koepke wanted to see if Newman could help him find the program *The 700 Club* producers were unable to find. Don called Newman.

Don recounted for Jerry the events of the last year to the present moment. Jerry was thrilled for Don. Don continued.

"Jerry, I have a question for you. I know you guys run *The 700 Club* regularly, right?"

"That's right," confirmed Newman.

"I was watching the program that night when I saw the interview with the alcoholic. Can you tell me what time you ran that show?"

There was dead silence on the other end. Now it was Jerry's turn to be baffled. Something was not adding up.

"Don, you said you were watching us airing *The 700 Club* at about 3 o'clock in the morning?"

"Yeah, that's right," Don affirmed.

"Uh, Don, you couldn't have been watching *The 700 Club* on our station."

"Why not?" asked a confused Koepke.

"Well, two good reasons," said Newman. "First, we're the only station to carry that program and we run that show at 10 o'clock in the morning. Second, we sign off the air at midnight!"

I Once Was Lost

Gary LaFave is the President and Executive Director of the Freedom House in Green Bay. This special ministry is a homeless shelter that can accommodate up to 15 families. Since 1992, Freedom House has served over 600 families including over 1,600 children. It offers programs that help families succeed in the spiritual, physical, emotional and financial areas of life. It's not glamorous work but, unfortunately, much needed and growing in demand.

As can be the case for non-profit organizations, funds were getting low at the Freedom House. Gary had thought for some time that what Freedom House needed was a spokesperson to help them in fundraising efforts, but who could they get? He certainly had his "wish list," but he knew that there would have to be divine intervention to pull off making that happen.

It was in January of 2005 that Gary began to seriously pray that God would send someone to help them with the financial aspects of Freedom House. Now, six months later, he was standing at a July press conference listening to a distinguished man making a plea for others to join him in an effort to keep the work of Freedom House alive. Gary was marveling at what God had done as the man spoke to the gathering from the media.

"I tell you that God led me here," he began. "I pray that you will join me in the effort here at the Freedom House. This is a wonderful ministry and I am proud to lend my name to it."

How did this gentleman, who was no stranger to anyone in Green Bay, find himself standing at the podium endorsing this ministry? Well, it seems that for the last six months, in one way or another, he kept hearing about the Freedom House.

His son came home from high school and said, "Hey, dad, in school today they were talking about the Freedom House and the homeless families in our community."

Then he read something in the paper about the Freedom House. Not long after that he heard something on the radio about the Freedom House. He had actually visited there back in 2000, but had not felt any sense of commitment to them at that time.

All these things made him wonder if he was, perhaps, destined to help in some way. He had, of course, convinced himself that he had a great excuse for not being involved. After all, he was incredibly busy and he gets thousands of requests to help other organizations and causes, so what was so special about this one? Then something happened to help him to reassess his thinking and future strategy.

It happened in July. He was on his way back to Green Bay from beautiful Door County, Wisconsin. He had spent some much-needed time relaxing, aware that his busiest time of year at work was on the horizon. Amazingly, some would say it was bizarre, he got lost in the Northeast part of Green Bay. Hardly a stranger to the community (he had lived there since 2000) he nevertheless was quite lost. He pulled into a parking lot in order to turn his car around, looked up and saw a sign that read, **Freedom House**. Next to the sign was a large building with a big white cross on the side of it.

"Okay, God, I get it!" he chuckled to himself as he headed his car in what he believed to be the right direction.

Arriving home safely, the "lost man" picked up the phone and contacted the Freedom House. The receptionist couldn't believe with whom he was speaking! The man requested a tour.

"When would you like to come over," asked the staff person.

"Would it be possible to come today?" he asked.

"Sure, come on over."

The tour went well, very well, in fact. He spent about two hours at the Freedom House chatting with families and getting to know more about the mission there. Before he left he had a simple but direct question.

"Do you need anything right now?"

"Yes, actually we do. We sure could use a large-screen TV."

"You'll have one within a week," the man declared without hesitation.

True to his word, the TV arrived within a week.

Now just six months after praying for someone to step forward and be a voice for the Freedom House, LaFave was attending this unbelievable press conference listening to this man address Green Bay and surrounding area media.

"I'm going to make the Freedom House an extension of my family," he told the media.

The man, no doubt, had any number of legitimate excuses to keep him from making any commitment to Freedom House or any of the thousands of other groups requesting help. He chose, nonetheless, to freely throw his hat in as an "official" spokesperson for the Freedom House, never questioning the divine orchestration that brought him to this particular moment in his life.

Who was this man "who once was lost," but now could be found at the Freedom House lending his name and resources? Well, the locals know him as the coach of a local team, a pretty popular team at that. There standing at the podium was none other than Mike Sherman, the head coach of the Green Bay Packers!

The Story of the Story

There's more to the story. The coach provided 33 tickets to the team's family night, 16 on the 50-yard line and 17 in his personal skybox at Lambeau Field. The topper for LaFave was when Coach Sherman asked if he could see Gary in the privacy of his office. He was quite clearly emotional before and while he spoke to Gary.

"I usually like to remain anonymous in things like this, but I want people to know that I would not ask them to support homeless families if I wasn't leading by example."

With that he handed LaFave a check for $50,000!

House for Sale

Pastor Larry and Carolyn Campbell answered the call to move and start a church in Columbus. It was January 1997. Making the move would require faith to find a house, not just any house, but a home where they could live and could accommodate several people at a time for Bible studies.

One day in April, Carolyn was praying for God to direct them to a house that He knew would be the right one for them. No sooner had the words left her mouth than she began to see a vision. It was similar to seeing a still picture on a television screen in her mind. She saw a white, ranch style home that seemed to be empty, perhaps because someone who had lived in it had recently passed away. Carolyn also had a sense that a school was five to six blocks from the home.

Almost every weekend Carolyn and Larry would make the two-hour trip from Clintonville to Columbus to go "house shopping." Carolyn had not shared the vision with Larry, which left him more than a bit puzzled as to why every search for a home began at a school and went five or six blocks out. Weekend after weekend they searched and still had not found a home that they were comfortable in making an offer to purchase.

Finally, knowing they needed to get to Columbus to begin their church, the Campbells chose a home to purchase, but it was not the one Carolyn had seen in her vision. She began to question if she had made a mistake, so they set up an appointment to look at the home one more time. On this trip the Campbells brought along some friends and a house inspector. Carolyn began to pray that God would reveal whether or not this was the house they were to live in.

"Lord, give me a spirit of unrest if this is not the house we are supposed to buy," she prayed.

More than once, while looking through the house, Carolyn would find herself wandering outside and just standing on the sidewalk, feeling extremely nervous and full of unrest. Ultimately, they decided not to buy that house, so the search continued.

Before continuing house hunting, the Campbells decided to show their friends around the city where they would soon be living. As they cruised around a few city blocks, Carolyn noticed a sign on a utility pole advertising an estate sale. Carolyn wondered if perhaps someone was selling their home because of a death in the family.

The sale was on Sunset Road. Thinking "Road" suggested the house would be out in the country Carolyn was concerned it would not be in town or close to schools as she had seen in her vision. As the Campbells drove on, suddenly they saw a street sign that read "Sunset Road!"

"Larry, we need to turn here!" Carolyn declared excitedly.

As they pulled up to the home, Carolyn was flabbergasted to see that this was the home in her vision!They got out of their car and a woman selling the personal property in the front yard greeted them. Carolyn made very little small talk as the woman explained that her mother, who had owned the house, had recently passed away. Certain that they had been led down Sunset Road, Carolyn knew exactly what she wanted to say.

"We'd like to buy your house!" said Carolyn.

The woman was startled by Carolyn's request. Carolyn had spoken with such an air of authority and conviction in her eyes that the woman couldn't help but respond immediately.

"Would you like to see it?" she asked.

"Yes, please!" replied Carolyn, now fully persuaded that this was the house God had shown her in April.

After a short tour of the home, the Campbells made an offer to purchase. It was accepted. Financing was approved and the story was complete, just the way Carolyn had envisioned it. The home was not only five to six blocks from a school, but it also had two things Carolyn had always desired in a home, a bathroom off the master bedroom and a screened in porch.

This story is just another example of God's faithfulness as far as the Campbells are concerned, but there was always something about the deal that perplexed Carolyn. More than once she had asked herself the same question since meeting the woman that day.

"I wonder why asking to buy the house was so startling to that woman? Why did she look so taken aback by our offer to buy it that day?"

Carolyn decided to recall all of the details in the January vision. Again, she saw the white ranch home that was now theirs. The vision became as clear as glass. She gasped in amazement as she noticed something for the very first time, something she had completely missed from the first vision.

The fact is there was *not* a **FOR SALE** sign in front of the house. As she thought back, she realized there was not a **FOR SALE** sign in front of the home the day they arrived at the estate sale either. It seems she had just *assumed* when she saw it, knowing it was the house from her vision, that it was for sale. It wasn't!

The Story of the Story

It's more than unusual, it's downright peculiar, to drive up to a home totally unannounced and offer to buy it.

Carolyn said that God had to arrange a few things before the deal to buy the house could be completed. For one thing, the appraisal did not come in at their offered price so, amazingly, the seller lowered the price another $5,000! And, rates hit a nice low on the day that the new home loan was approved. The home in Clintonville sold quickly, making for a seamless transition.

Larry and Carolyn faithfully served in Columbus until recently. Currently they are trusting God for the next step in their future. If there is any confusion as to where they are supposed to be next, no doubt God will give Carolyn a vision to help them.

Angels on the Dashboard

To this date he estimates he has driven at least 500,000 miles. What's especially astounding is that of all those miles, approximately 10,000 of them were while he was legally intoxicated until he got help for alcoholism April 15, 1991. Steven David believes it is by the grace of God that he has never been involved in a serious car accident.

Steven got his driver's license during his sophomore year of high school in April of 1976. His first car, a turquoise '65 Pontiac Catalina, had power steering and rode like a boat as it cruised down the highway. He had it just a few months when his dad bought him a blue-green '68 Chevy Impala with a four-barrel-carburetor.

Steven is the first to admit there have been several times when divine intervention was the only explanation for averted auto accidents, but the most significant was the night before Easter, 1978.

Steven had cut a date short with his girlfriend, Debbie, to go home to sleep off his exhaustion. As he was driving his banana yellow Dodge Charger home on U.S. Highway 45 between Eden and the family farm, a freezing drizzle began to fall. Steven nodded off a couple of times, but woke up each time as he hit gravel on the shoulder.

As he headed down a small incline of highway that eventually curved to the right, he fell asleep. Although he had been "out" for only three short seconds, when he snapped back the speedometer was reading 60 mph. Apparently when he fell asleep, he had accelerated!

Steven now realized he was losing control of the car's movement. He grabbed the wheel tightly in an effort to correct the car, but to no avail. It swerved to the right, to the left, and to the right again. Just ahead was the curve Steven intuitively knew he would never be able to negotiate under these conditions. Disaster was looming. At about 55 mph, the rear end of the car swung around to the right and headed straight for the ditch. Fortunately, there had been a thaw earlier that day, leaving the ditch muddy and slippery. With an almost slithering inertia, he slid down and into the ditch and then back up, spinning twice as he slid. He heard mud slapping up against the car as he thrashed through thicket after coming through the ditch.

Suddenly there was silence. The engine had died, but the dashboard and headlights remained lit. Steven's heart was pounding through his chest. He had survived. As he got out of the muddied car, he could feel the freezing rain slapping his face. What he saw next was amazing. Knowing that the roads he had just traveled for the past ten miles were laden with trees and stone fences all along the ditch line, he was immensely grateful. He realized that had he had this accident in any other place along this stretch of road, he most likely would be dead.

As he looked around, he saw that he was sitting right in the middle of a fifty by one hundred yard open area that had just been cleared in preparation for the development of a farm implement dealership!

The Story of the Story

The car started back up without any difficulty. Steven pulled into the driveway of the people who owned the property and got back on the highway. Once the initial shock wore off a bit, he realized that his aunt and uncle lived directly across the road. Not surprising, he had no trouble staying awake the rest of the way home, which was about two miles.

Grateful to be in one piece, Steven sprayed the car off by the barn and parked it in the shed. The next morning, after milking the cows, Steven's dad told him he could smell gasoline near the car. The incident from the night before had indeed punctured the gas tank. Steven concocted a half-baked explanation about what must have happened. When he returned to the house for breakfast after chores, his mom had just returned home from the Easter sunrise service. She had a casual comment for Steven.

"I see where someone ran into the ditch across from Uncle Norb's and Aunt Joyce's last night," she observed.

"Yeah, I saw that, too," he said.

Of course, those tracks were his. It wasn't until years later that he admitted the whole truth to his folks. Thank God for his angel on the dashboard who continues to watch over him. And I, Kathi Rose, count on that fact daily. You see, Steven David (Rose) is my husband and co-author of this book. This is just one of many "Godincidences" in his life.

Holy Soybeans!

*Caution: Please be sure that once you've read the story, you also read the disclaimer.

The fat lady was just about to sing. Steve Swan, a man of faith, was nearly done dancing. Farm Credit Services (FCS) had waited as long as they possibly could for the money that they had loaned to the Swans. FCS needed more than faith and promises from Swan, they needed cash. They had begun foreclosure on the Swan family farm in December of 2001.

This dilemma, soon to certainly be financial-family tragedy, had been brought on, in part, by Steve's over investment in the ginseng market. Steve, his wife Pam, and their family were involved in raising and selling Christmas trees. The fine details of this story are not as important as the facts of it, namely numbers. The faith of one man becomes a crucial part of the story, but let's start with the numbers.

Through divine networking, Steve Swan was able to contact Harlan Accola from Blue Jean Bankers in fall of 2001. Steve needed $330,000 to save the family farm. Literally, on the day that Farm Credit Services was going to be having a sheriff's auction to sell the Swan's farm, Steve and Harlan took a check to FCS and paid them off. But, it was merely a "stay of execution." There would need to be a few more miracles if the farm ultimately was going to be pulled out of the fire. So how, with poor credit, had Swan been able to find this help?

Through Harlan Accola's great connections and expertise, he was able to get Steve a risky, three-year "bridge loan." It was at an incredibly pricey 15% interest. The monthly payments alone were $5,000! The loan was backed up by the land and just about everything the Swans owned. His mother, Norma, had to sign off on her life estate on the land Steve's father had left him. The $330,000 loan bought some time and that's all Steve could hope for—for now, at least. You see, Steve believed God would deliver him from this financial burden.

Over the next three years, Steve made every monthly $5,000 payment. Many times it was tight, but he never missed one. Harlan learned that Steve was still dealing in the ginseng market and had some advice for him. Because of what he had been able to do to help Swan, Harlan felt he could share his concern and it would be received in the caring spirit in which Accola intended.

"Steve, here's the problem. You need to get out of the ginseng market!"

"But, God hasn't told me to get out yet," the somewhat naïve man of faith told Accola.

"Well, God told me to tell you to get out," said Accola not meaning to sound sarcastic. He was genuinely concerned for Steve and his family.

A month later, after praying about doing so, Steve did indeed get out of ginseng completely.

With more financial setbacks right after the Christmas tree season, there was only $20,000 left in discretionary, soluble funds. Steve had another challenging decision to make. He either needed to pay the note or come up with another "rabbit out of the hat," which didn't seem likely. Swan, however, remained optimistic.

"I really believe that God has given me a sign that He's gonna save the farm," he told Accola in late summer of 2004.

"I hope you're right, Steve," replied Accola. "If He doesn't come through, you can be assured that the investors of your loan will foreclose and take your land. That's one thing you can be certain of," he cautioned Swan.

Steve wandered back in his mind to a past prayer experience from 1998. Swan had held closely onto the details of it, sharing it only with a few select people. He had never told Harlan Accola. Although the Swans had been in the ginseng market, Steve believed the Lord told him in prayer that it would be soybeans, not ginseng or Christmas trees, that would save the farm. The whole soybean thing, however, always confused Steve primarily because he didn't know a thing about soybeans. Sometimes drastic times do call for drastic measures.

"If I'm going to lose the farm, what difference does it make? I'm going to take a chance," he thought to himself.

Steve went back to a time in prayer in 2002. He remembered something else from the day! He remembered asking the Lord something specific.

"God, if you want me to invest in soybeans send me a sign in the sky. If investing in soybeans is not the thing I need to do, show me what I should do," he prayed.

About three months later, Steve and his neighbor Jim were standing near a road on one of the farms when they heard a loud noise, which seemed to be the sound of turkeys coming out of the woods. The men were speechless. They looked up and about a quarter mile into the air were about 18 to 24 white eagles circling in a counter-clockwise direction. Inside the big circle were three eagles flying clockwise. That, to Steve, was the sign in the sky he was praying for! This confirmed in his heart and mind that it would be soybeans that saved the farm and the three eagles connoted to him that it meant he should purchase the soybeans in three years.

So, after much prayer, in February of 2005 that's what Steve did. He purchased 296 May Option contracts, the most risky kind that you can get. Amazingly, something incredible happened. In two-and-a-half weeks his $20,000 turned into $200,000! He got a call from his broker.

"Steve, sell your contracts. This never happens!" he told him.

"But, I need $350,000 to save the farm," he calmly told him. "I believe God is testing my faith," he told the broker.

Swan did not sell. The words of the stunned and panicked broker could have been haunting Swan as only a week later his soybean account went down about half, nearly $100,000. Certainly Swan would get out now? He didn't. He was patient. He had made the decision to stay the course. He needed $350,000 to save the farm and he believed, now more than ever, that God was going to deliver him from this financial challenge through soybeans, just as He had told him in prayer that He would.

About two weeks after the account spiraled downward, Swan phoned Accola.

"Harlan, I want to come down and pay off the loan," he said coolly. "What's the amount?"

"What, the $5,000?" Harlan asked.

"No, the whole amount," said Steve.

"What are you talking about?" he asked feeling quite confused and somewhat offended by the question. After all, how had Steve come up with $350,000?

"I have the money, Harlan. I just want to come down and pay off the note," he replied again calmly as though he were Jed Clampett.

Harlan decided to roll with the conversation and take the opportunity to educate Swan a little bit.

"Now, you realize, of course, that the investors aren't going to take a personal check, Steve. They're going to want certified funds," he said, still really in disbelief of Steve's request.

"That's fine. How do I do that?"

"Well, go to your bank and have them give you a certified check for the entire amount."

"All right. What time can we get together tomorrow?" asked Swan.

"Steve, I'm serious. Don't even think about coming down unless you have the money," he cautioned.

"I'll see you tomorrow."

Accola hung up the phone, shook his head in disbelief, and stared at his desk for some time before delving back into his pile of paperwork and phone calls.

The following morning, March 10, 2005, Harlan looked out of his office window and into the front lobby. There was Steve Swan. Harlan was more than curious to discover what was going on, especially if Steve really did have the money for the payoff. No doubt, there would be a good story. They gathered around the conference room table and Swan began to speak.

He went on to talk about the eagles and how he felt he would be purchasing soybeans three years after seeing the three eagles within the circle of eagles.

Nobody in that room had a clue what Swan was talking about, nor did they care. They wanted him to "show them the money."

Harlan and a few members of his staff continued to listen intently, if not still a bit skeptically.

"It didn't look good for a while there," said Swan in a ho-hum tone. "We gained and then lost a lot of money, but God is faithful and He always keeps His promises. This past week our investment really blossomed," he said with a grin from ear-to-ear, so wide he could have eaten a banana sideways.

With that comment, Swan reached into his pocket and began to lower a check onto the table. All eyes in the room, including those of "Doubting Harlan," looked down at it as it traveled in super-slow motion to the table surface. As it landed they could see numbers on it, lots of them.

Swan went on to tell them in his usual laid-back manner what had occurred just days before. Due to Steve Swan's childlike faith, patience and perseverance, in God's good and perfect timing, the Swan's soybean account that had been opened a month earlier, that had a total investment of about $20,000, had miraculously skyrocketed to $380,000! It was then, and only then, that Steve knew the Lord had freed him to sell his contracts, which he did. Soybeans had indeed saved the Swan family farm. Proof of that was the certified check that sat on the table for $352,185.00–the exact amount of the payoff of the bridge loan!

The Story of the Story

We have all the paperwork and details to verify this story. It is a wonderful testimony of what God can do when He chooses to test and honor a man's faith. This story is not to encourage anyone to do anything similar to what Steve Swan did, but rather to declare that God does, indeed, have a plan for each of our lives.

A Change of Heart

Where there is fun, one can usually find Joie Pirkey. Wherever Joie Pirkey is, there's some fun going on. The energetic mother of three has a love and zest for life. At age 36, Joie had enjoyed a life of great health and considered herself blessed. Little did she know that at the fateful stroke of midnight, literally, her health, her life and her world would do a complete one-eighty!

It was June 27, 2000, when Joie's sister, Annie, was celebrating her 25th birthday. The family had gathered at the Silver Spur in Darboy. Along with lots of good food and refreshments, there was great music. The clock had just struck midnight when, while dancing, Joie suddenly began experiencing excruciating pain in her jaw. Electrical impulses shot through her chest. The pain became unbearable.

Joie got dizzy and became nauseated, as if she was coming down with a nasty case of the flu. With each second the pain in her jaw grew worse, until it felt like a "toothache from hell." The pain dropped from her jaw to underneath her right collarbone.It felt as if someone had driven an ice pick into her chest and was clamping down like a vise.

Barely conscious, Joie knew something was very wrong. Having gone through childbirth three times, she knew that this pain was clearly not "natural."

"Call 9-1-1!" someone yelled.

Paramedics arrived quickly and immediately transported her to the nearest hospital. Soon Joie was the subject of chaos and commotion at St. Elizabeth's Hospital. She had suffered a heart attack. Doctors were stumped. There was no history of heart disease in the family. It made no sense to Joie either, a lifelong athlete who had always been in remarkably good health. Now she was fighting for her life. As she lay in I.C.U. she had a question go through her mind.

"God, do you know this is happening to me?"

Just then, she saw in a vision a cross on the wall and could feel a Presence enter the room. A gentle calm came over her. Then she had something else pop into her mind.

"I'm not good enough to get to heaven," she uttered, a sudden panic setting in.

"But Jesus is!" she heard a voice say to her.

"Are you going to heal me?" she asked of the unseen Someone who was conversing with her in her mind.

"When you see the white bird," was all she heard.

She had no idea what that meant. For the moment, she was just glad to know she was living. But, the news got worse before it got better. The following day at 3 p.m. Joie had another heart attack. That episode left her in very critical condition. Prayer and faith kept her alive, but the following days were tense for Joie and her family.

Late in the afternoon, Joie was transferred to University Hospital where she was diagnosed with Coronary Vasospasm. This disease caused the arteries in the heart to spasm randomly, depriving the heart of oxygen, which caused a heart attack. Joie would experience spasms five or six times a day. Eventually they tapered to about once every three days. Still, every time Joie would have a spasm, she never knew if her current breath was going to be her last. Then came the national disaster of 9-11, which didn't help stress levels, either.

Doctors kept Joie medicated, but they also told her in no uncertain terms that she was a walking time bomb, that the next heart attack would most likely kill her and it was just a matter of time. By God's grace Joie made it to see the year 2001 come in. That January, after a year of unsuccessful treatment, she was referred to a heart specialist, Dr. Charles Bruce, at the Mayo Clinic in Rochester, MN. The news he gave her was no more encouraging than other doctors had given her.

"Joie, you do, as you know, have Coronary Vasospasm," he began. "You have one of the most aggressive cases that we've ever seen. Because there is no cure for this disease, finding the right combination of medication is your only hope," said Dr. Bruce. "But, uh, you can only have so many heart attacks..." he mumbled in a barely audible voice, hoping maybe Joie hadn't heard him.

She had.

Shortly after this news she and her family were also informed that there was a dangerous procedure necessary to find the right combination of medication to help control her condition. The test would also help to determine if the disease was hereditary, and whether or not her children may have been stricken as well.

Whether there would be a form of medication that would help her or not, Joie knew where she stood. With each spasm her heart was getting weaker. If the disease was incurable, there was one responsible thing she needed to do. In April, she planned her funeral, picked out her songs, the whole nine yards. She did ask her doctors one more question.

"How can I adjust to this?"

Again, she received another less-than-satisfactory answer.

"You need to adjust to not being able to adjust," Dr. Geller, cardiologist from St. Elizabeth's Hospital, told her.

Joie heard what the doctors had said, but she also heard something in her spirit that reminded her that everyone was going to die, some sooner, some later. Time and more of God's continued grace held her fragile heart and her life together. Joie had decided to schedule the risky test at the Mayo Clinic, which was set for October 10.

Ten days prior to the appointment, on September 30, coincidently at the same time as her first heart attack, at midnight, Joie had a vision! She and Douglas had retired for the night when, suddenly, she began to see through her ceiling as if into the heavenlies. Off to the left side of the vision Joie saw a short man wearing a robe with a crown atop his head. He lowered it to Joie showing her the top of it. She was able to talk with Douglas the whole time the vision was playing out. Before she could count the number of points on the crown, the man moved away and there appeared a white dove. Then it hit her.

"You will be healed when you see the white bird!" she recalled from a year earlier.

There was no doubt in Joie's mind that those words were the same words she heard from the Spirit of God as she lay dying fifteen-months earlier at St. E's Hospital the night of the heart attack. Because this vision was so powerful and deeply personal, it was virtually impossible for Joie to describe it. The fact is something had happened to her and she intuitively knew she *had* been healed.

However, compelled by a deep desire to know for certain, Joie and Douglas decided to keep the appointment at the Mayo Clinic. She also decided to wean herself from her medication in three days, which concerned the doctors at the Mayo Clinic when she told them.

"I want you to know that I'm healed," Joie told the doctors just before they began the test. They were gracious, but cynical.

A super-specialist administered the procedure and was the first to tell Dr. Bruce what he had found, who then spoke to Joie and Douglas. He looked a bit shaken, quite puzzled, even disturbed.

"Uh, we have good news," he began. "Great news, actually. I talked with Dr. Amir who did the test. First of all, you have no signs of Coronary Vasospasm. Furthermore, your heart is free from all the plaque build-up that had been apparent on two previous angiograms."

Although Joie and Douglas were not surprised, they were, nonetheless, thrilled to have their faith affirmed. Dr. Bruce had one more statement.

"When we judge the strength of a heart, the benchmark is that of a male in his twenties. Well, your heart is even *stronger* than that…we'd have to say your heart is Super-Normal!"

The Story of the Story

"We have a verifiable, documented miracle," were Dr. Bruce's final words.

Today, Joie is healthy and happy as ever and has no recurrence of any signs of heart disease.

Joie Pirkey is a walking miracle, and a living testimony to the power of the Lord, to whom she gives all thanks and praise.

A Lucky Brake?

Greg and Janet Rajala had been married almost three years in the spring of 1977 when they moved from St. Paul, Minnesota to Milwaukee, Wisconsin. Greg had taken a new job at Bucyrus-Erie Company where he designed heavy mining equipment.

The Rajalas had grown up in the same general area in northern Wisconsin and northern Michigan, so during this phase of their marriage they often took weekend trips back home to hunt, fish or to visit friends and family. It was on a Friday when one of those trips was scheduled to take place. In order to save some travel time, Janet had an idea.

"Greg, why don't I drop you off at work so I can run some errands and then pack for the trip?" she suggested.

"That's a good idea," agreed Greg.

Janet drove their '67 Buick Skylark the six-mile trek from their apartment to Greg's office. Greg was looking forward to the upcoming trip.

"This work day is going to go by far too slowly," he told Janet. "Let's pack some sandwiches so we don't have to stop on the way."

"Sounds fine to me," said Janet. In fifteen minutes it was time to say goodbye for a few hours.

"I'll pick you up after work," she told her husband.

"I'll be waiting for you," Greg assured her.

That afternoon Janet got gas for the car, had the oil checked and went to the post office. She also bought some groceries and a gift for her sister. When she got home, she packed all the necessary things for the weekend away. She wrapped a few sandwiches and filled the thermos bottle with coffee. Then she packed the car with the luggage and food.

Coming back into the apartment one last time, she glanced up at the kitchen clock. The activities had taken Janet longer than she had planned and so she was running a bit behind. As she prepared to lock up and leave the apartment, she felt rushed and flustered, so she took a few minutes to kneel by the couch and say a prayer.

"Dear heavenly Father. I thank you for what you have given us…I also ask that you would provide for a smooth trip and safety along the road. In Jesus' name, Amen."

Janet started the car and was headed down the steep driveway of the apartment. She took a right onto 23rd Street and then a left onto College Avenue. She proceeded through three sets of lights, then took a right onto 13th Street. Turning left on Rawson Avenue, she headed to South Milwaukee and Greg's office. About halfway there, Janet suddenly realized she needed to return to the apartment.

"Oh, my goodness! I forgot the gift for my sister!" she exclaimed to herself.

She turned around and headed back the same way she had come. She pulled into the parking stall, ran into the apartment for her sister's gift and returned to the car. As she prepared to back out of the parking stall by depressing the brake pedal in order to put the car in gear, the brake pedal had no pressure whatsoever. It went all the way to the floor! She immediately turned off the car and called her husband.

"Honey, something is wrong with the car. Can you get a ride home?"

"I'll be home as quickly as I can," he told Janet.

A friend, Tom Williams, gave Greg a ride home in his '67 VW Beetle.

"Thanks for the ride, Tom," Greg told his friend as he got out of the vehicle.

"Have a great weekend," he told Greg.

Greg went over to the car and began to inspect it. To his surprise and horror, one of the rubber hoses that formed the flexible connection between the rigid brake lines and front brakes was broken. He then looked under the hood to discover there was very little brake fluid left in the reservoir and hardly any sign of brake fluid on the ground. Apparently all the brake fluid had been pumped out of the system by Janet's use of the brakes in the course of her day's travels. The last ounce of brake fluid had gotten pumped out as his wife parked the car at the apartment!

Although their trip was going to have to be postponed, the Rajalas found no reason for disappointment, but were instead grateful. Greg put his arm around Janet as their eyes looked at the car with no brakes. Then, almost simultaneously, they both turned and stared down the steep driveway from the apartment to the busy street below.

"What if? Oh, my God, what if?" whispered Greg to his wife.

The Story of the Story

Greg and Janet Rajala went on to live a happy and fulfilling life, eventually raising six children together, until May of 2000, when Janet was tragically killed in a traffic accident.

Lyons Can't Fly

It's a deer hunter's prayer, a light snow falling the night before opening day to help "track" the prize. Well, that's what was happening near Gillett on the eve before the opening day of deer season, November 18, 1995.

Bob Lyons and a few of his friends set out to get their trophies opening morning. They had some breakfast, grabbed their gear and headed for the woods.

They wished each other luck as they split up to various parts of the woods. Bob sat out at one of his stands for the better part of the morning, but decided to move around lunchtime to something deeper in the woods.

Bob had no sooner set out when he came upon another tree stand. Although the group had done extensive bow hunting together in this location before, Bob had never seen this particular stand until today.

"I wonder why it's up so high?" he questioned before deciding it would be a great place to get above the scent of the deer.

The tree had huge railroad spikes in the trunk that served as a kind of stepladder to the stand. Bob's rifle was empty and the safety was set. He found a rope at the base of the trunk that someone had left behind. Bob tied it around his gun so that he could pull it up to himself once he had arrived in the stand.

Bob began the nearly 35-foot ascent. Midway in the climb, he suddenly realized that he had left his safety strap at the stand he had been sitting at earlier that morning, but going back for it was not a viable option. After a few more minutes of exhaustive climbing, Bob found himself near the base of the stand, but unable to get up into it.

"Whew, why am I so tired?" he wondered as he rested for a moment.

Although it was November in Wisconsin, he was perspiring profusely. Bob then noticed that the last two railroad spike steps closest to the base of the stand were missing. He concluded that he would have to get some lift from his knees and feet to propel himself up into the stand. Bob knew that there was little room for error, but he'd had similar challenges before, so he discounted the potential danger.

Bob took a deep breath, sprung upward and grabbed for the stand. He was not able to reach it, but did manage to keep his balance and composure on the spikes.

"I'll rest for a minute and try this one more time," he reasoned. "If I don't make it the next time, I'm out of here!" he thought to himself.

Bob looked at the stand to make sure there was no snow on the surface of it that would cause his hands to slip. He saw nothing. Bob took another deep breath and sprung up and to his right. His hands grasped the base of the stand, but as he tried to pull himself up, his belt caught on the corner of the stand. It brought him to an abrupt halt, and then he lost his grip on the stand. Bob knew instantly that he was in deep trouble!

Although the sequence of events took a mere few seconds, everything seemed to be happening in slow motion.

First, he pushed himself away from the tree to avoid hitting the spikes.

"Lord, I'm in your hands now," he thought as he began his rapid descent back down to earth.

Then Bob hit what felt like something solid before he actually hit the ground and was knocked unconscious. When he finally woke, he was startled and disoriented.

"Why in the world did I take a nap here?" he wondered.

Slowly he began to recall the events that led to his falling from the tree.

"Why don't I feel any pain?" he questioned as he lay on the soft bed of snow. He surmised he had been out for some time because when he had fallen it was overcast, now it was sunny.

Assuming he was all right, Bob started to get up. Suddenly he couldn't breathe! Injury from the fall compounded with asthma made it a dangerous situation. He lay back down and then phoned for help. One of the first responders looked up in the tree and couldn't believe what he saw.

"It's a miracle he's not dead!" he said more to himself than aloud.

Nearly an hour had passed since the mishap. Bob was transported by ambulance to the Shawano Hospital. Upon arrival, Randy, one of the fellow hunters, called Pastor John Hoppe who then called Bob's wife, Mary, to tell her of the accident. Meanwhile, Bob was given morphine to minimize the intensity of the pain he was now experiencing.

A CT scan determined that there were no major internal, spinal or cervical injuries, which was a miracle. He had, however, suffered a compound fracture to his clavicle, four fractured ribs on the right side and numerous contusions to the midsection of his body. The EMT's initial reaction was accurate—it was a miracle that he was alive.

One of the EMTs noted that the fatality rate for anyone falling from the height of twenty feet or more is 80%. Bob amazingly had survived a fall of thirty-five feet.

"How could this be?" wondered both doctors and the responders. Needless to say, they were clearly amazed, and suspected that Bob had something "working for him."

Bob spent only a few days in the hospital mending, but during his stay he had two interesting dreams on consecutive nights. In each dream he could feel himself falling from the tree stand. Each time he flinched and woke abruptly, doubled over in pain. Each night he looked at the clock. It was exactly 3 a.m. Each time a nurse came in after hearing his groans and administered pain medication.

Bob got some great news on Wednesday the 22nd of November. He was to be released. Not only would he be able to spend Thanksgiving with his family, but he knew that this year, especially, he had much for which to be thankful.

Mary and the children, Nicole, Matt, and Sean, took great pains to make Thanksgiving special. They, too, had hearts full of gratitude for Bob's return home. After a late turkey dinner with all the trimmings the kids went to bed, leaving Mary and Bob the only ones still up.

Mary was in the kitchen doing the supper dishes when Bob realized it was time for another pain pill and he had left his medication on the kitchen counter. He took his pills and decided to sit and chat with Mary awhile before retiring for the night.

"Mary, I've got to tell you something. I had two very peculiar dreams while I was in the hospital," he said.

"Really? What happened?"

"Well, in each one I felt myself falling from the tree again. It seemed so real and downright scary! Just as I was about to hit the ground I woke up, doubled over in pain. Each night the nurse heard me yell and came in to make sure I was all right and to give me something for the pain," he said.

Mary's face was one of shock as she looked over at Bob.

"What nights did you have those dreams?" she questioned.

"It was both Sunday and Monday nights," he answered.

She was silent for a moment, then said pensively, "Each morning at exactly 3 a.m., Matt woke up from having had a dream. He said that in each dream he saw you falling from the tree, but there were four angels breaking your fall before you hit the snow!"

Saved by Fire

The Clementi family's church attendance was one. The one who "warmed" the pew was Lorraine Clementi. Her prayer was that her husband, Tony, would join her there. On May 5, 2005, however, she found herself with a totally different prayer need.

A man clearing his land let a small fire get out of control. It escalated into a 4,000-acre forest fire, forcing more than 135 families from their homes. The fire tore through several communities destroying 30 homes and 60 mobile homes and other structures. Thankfully no one was injured.

' Lorraine and Tony Clementi were one of the families whose home was in the path of the fire. She was bringing her granddaughter, Echo, home from a doctor's visit when, about 20 miles from her home, she could see the smoke. She knew a huge fire was raging near her home. There was only one solution to her problem and that was to pray. Immediately she pulled off the highway.

"Oh Dear God, I pray for Your Holy Angels to encamp around our home and valuables and to protect it," prayed Lorraine.

To make matters more harrowing, the Clementi's property was not insured.

By the time she reached their driveway, the fire was less than two miles away. Firemen and police made her turn and leave without her pets. Lorraine phoned her husband, Tony, at work. They had no idea where to go so they decided that they would meet at the McDonalds in Adams. Their daughter, Lisa, met them there about a half-hour later. She had heard on the radio that victims of the fire were meeting at Pineland Grade School. That's where the Clementis went.

Tony and Lorraine sat and listened as DNR officials confirmed their worst fear. Their home was in the path of the fire! Lorraine didn't lose faith, however, and spoke aloud to the group.

"I know our house is safe. Echo and I prayed and I know that God and His angels are protecting our home," she proclaimed unwaveringly to those at the school.

The Clementis then decided that they would head to the Chula Vista Hotel to spend the evening while they waited to find out their fate from the fire. It was during the drive that her husband made a somewhat sarcastic comment. Lorraine paid close attention to it, but held her ground.

When the fire was extinguished and the smoke cleared the Clementis were allowed to go back to their home. They found that their home, cars, and pets were all fine! It appeared that there had been a protective bubble around their property. Others in the neighborhood lost everything, but, for some reason, the Clementi's property was barely touched by the flames!

There were now two Clementis in church. Tony, who had for years chosen not to attend with his wife, was now sitting next to Lorraine. And it was all because of the snide comment he had made during the drive to the hotel. What exactly had he said?

"If our house is safe, I will believe and go to church with you!"

The Story of the Story

God does have a great sense of humor. Lorraine stood in front of the congregation that day and proclaimed, "We didn't have fire insurance on our home, but we had "God" insurance!"

Many properties in the neighborhood had significant damage. A closer look of the area did indeed show a "bubble" around the Clementi homestead. The only damage was to the garage. Strangely enough, inside of it were a couple of empty LP gas tanks that could have blown up the neighborhood, but the tanks were not touched by the flames!

By the way, this is the second time that the Clementis were protected. Lorraine's prayer for the "protective bubble" proved true to form when they were spared damage from a tornado nearly 10 years ago. Grandson Wayne has talked about "Grandma's protective bubble" ever since the tornado. Who is going to refute it?

Alphonso's Dream

In May of 1985, Alphonso James was a 16-year-old uneducated, poor, African American champion break-dancer, and a pronounced "tough guy" in his Milwaukee neighborhood. He lived with an anger that left him "on the edge" most of the time. If you knew his family story, you would understand just why an ordinary day included cruising, hanging out with thugs, looking for trouble and usually finding it. He had enemies. He never knew when he would be the target of a gang lookin' for him.

A few weeks earlier he'd been involved in a fight with a rival gang. Tempers flared, knives and fists were drawn, and blood was shed, though no one was mortally injured.

"Fons, we'll get you," declared a rival gang member as he fled bleeding profusely from a knife wound inflicted by AJ. The local hospital was known for their constant availability to treat the Milwaukee "gun and knife club."

So you can understand that there was incredible tension for AJ who was living with his head on a swivel, always expecting a snake under every rock. It would have been bad enough to be living in the inner city, never knowing where his next meal was coming from, but there were these concerns, too. Welcome to "Alphonso's world."

AJ lived with his mom, Julia, in the family's "turn around and see yourself" home. When it came time to go to sleep for the night a broken down couch served as his resting place in the living room where the picture window faced the street.

One particular night, for some reason, mom sat in a chair alongside of him as he slept. She couldn't help but notice her boy's chest heaving and his body twitching throughout the night. Then she spotted a car parked on the street outside the home.

In no time, four teenage boys exited the vehicle, leaned against it while gaping at the James' house.

"What's going on?" wondered Julia. "Who are those kids?"

The entire time that they stood outside, it was clear they were contemplating something and, in Julia's mind, it wasn't good. After about an hour, at approximately 3 a.m., they got back in their car and quickly left. Had they seen something? Had they been frightened off? Who knows, but they were gone and mom, for one, was relieved.

The sun began to break through bringing a new day with it, but AJ was still twitching and reeling as he slept. Finally an exhausted Alphonso woke. He felt as though he hadn't slept a wink. A nightmare had literally robbed him of all his rest. He didn't think too much of it at the time, but it came back to haunt him later that day.

Here's what he dreamed. He saw a vision in his mind, much like a split screen. On the left side he saw himself dead in a casket. He was laid out in the only decent outfit he owned. It was frightening, of course, because even though he was always aware that he had enemies, he did feel somewhat invincible. On the other side of the "screen" vision he saw a god-awful place with cement walls and bars. The atmosphere was heavy and evil. He had never seen this place before and was sure that he never wanted to again. Although he was tempted, he decided not to tell anyone about his dream.

On July 26, 1985, just two months later, two policemen arrived at his front door, insisting that he come downtown to talk with them. He assumed it was about the stabbing. It wasn't. It was about murder! Although he was wide-awake, AJ found himself in the middle of a real-life nightmare.

"I stabbed somebody a couple months ago," he admitted, "But I didn't kill nobody!" Alphonso proclaimed. Alphonso, scared out of his wits, was interrogated by detectives for hours, threatened and tricked into signing a piece of paper that turned out to be a confession.

For months this young man sat in jail with his very life hanging in the balance while he waited for trial. He could not imagine how he could be convicted. Because he hadn't done it there would be no evidence.

"But what if?" he thought from behind locked doors.

In February of 1986 a three-day trial ended after minimal testimony that included eyewitnesses who didn't tell the truth and unenthused personal counsel who barely cross examined the prosecution's witnesses. AJ's greatest fear became his reality, a guilty verdict. Now, he'd be torn from his freedom, family and most painful of all, a new baby daughter named Shakkarish. Alpshonso was sentenced to life in prison.

One nightmare flowed into the next as he was taken north to Green Bay Correctional Institution. He exited the vehicle in shackles, was led through an open door that slammed behind him, and then was processed. And then, he witnessed something strange. He saw cement walls and bars, the exact ones he had seen in his dream that summer, although it meant nothing to him at the time.

The first few years of incarceration were pure hell. Learning to survive prison environment fueled James' deep-seated anger. Chaplain Paul Emmel began to visit AJ regularly while he was in segregation.

"Alphonso, God loves you and has a plan for your life," he would tell him.

AJ didn't want to hear it. Quite frankly, without getting into detail, he said and did things to this man of God that no one would have done to his worst enemy. Chaplain Emmel, however, kept coming back day after day, week after week, and month after month, always with the same message.

"Alphonso, God loves you and so do I," he told him. "Here's a Bible for you."

What Alphonso was too proud to admit to Chaplain Emmel was that he couldn't read.

Sometimes pride can be a powerful motivator.

AJ got a dictionary from a prison library cart. He taught himself to read that Bible.

"After ten years of never giving up on me, Chaplain Emmel had loved the hate away from me." AJ had had a powerful spiritual awakening!

Now a renewed man, no longer in fights, dealing drugs or leading the gangs from the inside, he was doing and seeing things quite differently. Many found it strange to see him reading his Bible and praying.

Shortly after his conversion experience, Alphonso found himself chatting with a fellow inmate. Actually they were serious enemies ten years earlier in Milwaukee. What the man told James provided an incredible revelation.

"Fonso," he began. "One night after we had it out wit' you guys, the boys and me was outside your crib. We was there most uf da night. We was gonna come in an' kill you!" he confessed.

It was then Alphonso realized his dream of '85 had come full circle. Nearly ten years later, he now caught what God was trying to tell him.

Remember that in the right side of the vision he saw the god-awful place with bars? That was identical to the site he saw when he entered the Green Bay Prison! Although falsely convicted, he was alive.

If you recall, in the left side of his dream he'd seen himself in a casket. Apparently that was exactly what the devil had planned for him the night the "bad guys" were waiting outside the James house in 1985!

Story of the Story

The last 20 years have been incredibly difficult, to say the least, but AJ remains convinced that prison did indeed save his life. He stands firm on Chaplain Emmel's claim that God has a powerful plan for his life, regardless of where he may spend that life.

We've known Alphonso James since May of 2001. After Steve spoke to the inmates in the Oshkosh Correctional Institution, AJ introduced himself and shared his story. The Innocence Project in Madison is pursuing an appeal of Alphonso's conviction. He is currently awaiting exoneration while serving at the Stanley Correctional Institution.

Follow the Little Blue Truck

The weather on July 4, 1999, was hot and humid. Joe and Heide Schraufnagel and family had spent a relaxing day at a campground in north central Wisconsin. It was their hope to spend an equally quiet evening there as well. Those plans went "south" when at 7:30 p.m. severe weather engulfed the area. Tornado warning sirens blared as Joe made the decision to head for safety at their lake home just a few miles away.

"Let's get to the cottage. We'll be safer there," he insisted.

Piling into the car were children Katy and Brian, and Heide's mother, Peg. Joe was at the wheel. Rain pelted the windshield like BBs as they sped down the highway and came to an intersection. Joe sat idle at a stop sign they had been at numerous times before. This time, however, he noticed something very strange. The road that led straight ahead to the cottage wasn't there! Although it was 7:45 p.m., dark and overcast, five sets of eyes had the same report. No road! Then Heide had a rationalization.

"Maybe it's flooded out?"

"Heide, there's no road!" said Joe looking through the raindrops. Admittedly, he was confused, even somewhat spooked, and totally at a loss for words.

They sat for several minutes at the stop sign trying to determine how to get to the cottage. Suddenly, appearing as if out of nowhere, without a sound or glare from the headlights in their rear view mirror, was a truck. It pulled up along the left side of the Schraufnagel's car. It was a Ford F-150 that looked as though it had more than a few miles on it. A beautiful blonde woman, who appeared to be in her forties, rolled down the passenger window of the truck. She seemed to be delighted to see them.

"Oh, you're the Schraufnagels!" she called out, as if she had known them forever.

Everyone in the car was baffled as to why the woman none of them had ever met knew who they were. Without hesitation, or allowing Joe to speak, she had some instructions.

"Just follow me," she yelled. "When I wave you on, just keep going, all right?" she commanded as she pulled away in front of them.

"But, how do you know where we are going?" yelled Joe to the woman who paid no attention to him whatsoever.

The truck took a left at the intersection and, with nothing but "blind trust," Joe began to follow her. It was then that a quick poll was taken and Peg, for one, was worried.

"What are you doing? We don't know who she is?" she warned. "How does she know where we are going? I'd turn around if I were you!"

Brian and Katy were also expressing concern and fear, but they were at the mercy of mom's and dad's decision. The fact that the woman called them by name gave Joe enough of a "gut" feeling to follow her.

The first peculiar event was that, as soon as they began to follow her, the rain seemed to ease up making it easier to see. Joe assumed that the woman was leading them to their cottage, but he wasn't sure. He became even more confused as she led them down unknown, winding roads in all directions. It didn't take them long to realize they were going on sheer trust—totally. Still, they continued to follow directly behind her.

Then, on a somewhat straight stretch of highway, the woman's left arm appeared out of the window and, as she had promised, she motioned in a forward sweeping manner alerting them to go straight. She, however, turned left. No sooner did she do so than all five in the car saw the same thing. The truck appeared to vanish! No headlights were to be seen, no taillights, no flashes of blue, nothing! Granted, it was still raining and getting darker, but—poof—she was gone and they all saw it.

Now, really "freaked out," Joe sped up as the rain began to pour down even harder than before. Suddenly, he and Heide noticed that they were nowhere near the cottage at all, but were, in fact, coming in on an unfamiliar road that brought them back to the campground! From the second they got out of the car it began to rain the hardest it had all night.

The bewildered family spent little time talking about what had just happened. For the moment, it was enough to focus their energies on finding a way to stay safe in the midst of the storm. But, the night's events were certainly not far from any of their minds.

With a clear morning came an opportunity to look around. There were downed branches everywhere and other kinds of damage from Mother Nature's rage the night before. After a healthy breakfast they packed their belongings again, determined to go to the cottage.

Joe led them back on the same highway they had taken the night before. In minutes they found themselves at the exact same stop sign as previously. This time, however, there was a new mystery to try to understand.

"Oh, my God, Heide. Look, the road goes through!" blurted Joe.

"What is going on?" was the instant question on everyone's mind.

For some reason, now the road went through whereas just the night before it had not! So through the intersection they went on the "road that was not before" until Joe observed something ahead of them lying on the road.

"Oh, wow, look at that!" he blurted aloud.

The area was a mess, strewn with debris everywhere, like a bona fide disaster area. What they saw next brought simultaneous terror and a revelation. Stretched across the full width of the road "that didn't exist" was a huge tree. It was at least three feet in diameter. It was the type of obstacle that could have been deadly if it had caught a traveler by surprise. A car going 40 to 50 miles an hour during a rainstorm would have been no match for its destructive power. Joe and Heide just looked at each other. No words were exchanged, but there was a "knowing" that passed between them.

Soon everyone in the car seemed to be getting a revelation about the bizarre happenings of the night before. Joe, Heide, Peg, Katy and Brian unanimously agreed they indeed owed "someone" a debt of gratitude. They now knew that if not for a road that had conveniently vanished, and a beautiful blonde in an old blue Ford-150, there was a significant chance that the road they had wanted to drive on the night before may have led them to a serious disaster and potential tragedy. There was even the possibility that no one would have lived to tell this story!

Ring Around the Clams

Dr. Stewart Petrie, 82, and his wife, Mary, 64, have been married thirty-eight years. They met while he was a doctor and she was a nurse. He treasures not only her, but also the symbol of their love that she gave to him the day they married, September 10, 1967.

So, each time Stewart went clamming in the waters near their home he always took his wedding ring off—well, almost always. There was one regrettable exception in late July, 2003. It was on that day the former doctor had waded out in the waters of the Long Island Sound, off Indian Neck, and he realized his mistake.

"Aw, I forgot to take my ring off," he thought to himself.

He decided that he'd just take his chances rather than trudge back to shore to take it off. He proceeded to take his clamming rake further into the water. He did snag a few that day and took them home, which was just across the street.

It wasn't until he was home when he noticed his left hand felt odd.

"Mary, my wedding ring is gone!" he exclaimed.

He traced the steps of his day in his mind very quickly, and could only come to one conclusion. Apparently, the cold water had shrunk his finger and the ring had fallen off into the murky four-foot deep water. Understandably, he felt awful about it. And that feeling stayed with him for a long time.

On July 19, 2005, Dr. Petrie made his way out about 20-yards off shore to practice his sport again. A clamming rake is about 4-feet long with five or six prongs on the end of it. As he scraped the sandy floor underneath he brought clams to the surface and put them in his basket.

He had barely settled into the kitchen to begin to clean the clams when he noticed something in his basket of clams.

"Honey, look at this," he told Mary. "It's a ring."

"Wouldn't it be funny if it was your ring?" his wife quipped skeptically.

Mary scrubbed it with jewelry cleaner and dried and polished it. An inscription on the inside became obvious. It read:

MPS to SJP 9-10-67

Dr. Petrie had made the ultimate catch of all!

The Story of the Story

"It was an absolutely stupendous feeling," said Dr. Petrie upon realizing the ring was his.

We watched this story on our local news shortly after it happened.

"Honey, that's a story we should have in our book," Steve said.

We forgot about it for a month. Then just before the book was completed in late August, we did a search on the Internet for "Stewart Petrie." We prayed, "God, if you want this story in our book, You'll facilitate talking with him." Within ten minutes Steve was talking with both Dr. and Mrs. Petrie in their home in Branford, Connecticut!

After talking with Dr. Petrie, Steve came to the conclusion, knowing nothing about clamming, by the way, that there was one big miracle. Dr. Petrie explained to Steve that it's not unusual for there to be 6-7 foot tides along the shore where he clams. So how, after two years, was the ring still there, in the same location as where he had lost it? Stewart told Steve that he clammed an area about the size of a football field. The ring must have become embedded quickly under the sand after it landed in the water. That was the only fair assumption either of us could make. Regardless, this is another great story about how God can redeem a man's mistake.

There is one "bonus" to the story that didn't hit the news. The Petries have a grandchild they had not talked with in over five years who heard the story and contacted them. That incident alone confirmed what we have said for some time, "God is the greatest networker in the world!"

Don't Mess with Cassie

Cassie Chivers is a teenager who packs a wallop wherever she goes. This has nothing to do with her size, but Who she knows. Brought up in rural USA by God-fearing parents, she had the blessing of coming into the faith as a little girl. It was then that she asked God to use her to do something big, not just anything, but something extraordinary. She promised Him that He would get lots of glory. Have you ever heard the phrase, "Be careful what you pray for, you might get it." Maybe that applies to the life and story of Cassie Chivers.

Charlie and Debbie Chivers had started a ministry in 1982 called Special Touch. The organization ministers to those with disabilities. As much as the Chivers love to help others, clearly God and family are their top priorities, so when any of their daughters has questions or needs help, they are there for them.

On February 6, 2004, the entire Chivers family was in Madison staying at the Comfort Inn, preparing to do a Special Touch Retreat. A national newscast announced the upsetting news that the body of an abducted Florida girl, Carlie Bruscia, had been found. The news prompted their middle daughter, Cassie, 13, to ask her father a question.

"Dad, what do I do if someone puts a gun to my head and tries to take me away?" she asked.

"Honey, you fight, kick, scream, and do whatever you can to get away," he answered.

Later that day a young girl was sent out to do an errand from the same hotel. She got on an elevator. She didn't think anything unusual about the man who got on the elevator with her. He made "small talk" with her during the elevator ride. When they got to the second floor the man spoke.

"Why don't you go first?" he motioned to the girl in a gentlemanly gesture.

As she stepped out the door, the man crept up behind her, and put his hand over her mouth and a gun to her temple!

"If you scream, I'll blow your brains out," he threatened.

As he began to drag her away, she intuitively knew the man was going to rape her.

She struggled to pry his fingers away from her mouth to take a breath. When she finally took that breath, she used it to pray out loud, "God, I love you, God you're so awesome!"

"Shut up!" he told the teenager as she prayed.

As he dragged her down the fire escape, the young lady helplessly heard her family talking and laughing through the wall. She wondered if she would ever see her family again. That was when God told her in her heart to trust Him, that He had it under control. She made the decision that she was not going to go with the man.

"He can shoot me, but that's okay, because I know I'm going to go to heaven," she thought to herself.

The thug took her to an alley where his intentions certainly were going to be far from anything honorable. About 100-feet away, she saw her friends, who had just arrived at the hotel for the retreat. She doesn't recall what happened next, other than she was screaming and running to her friends. Thinking she was going to be shot in the back any moment, she looked back at the man only once and all she saw was the back of his head.

"At that point, I knew I had won," she told authorities.

Shortly after the kidnapping attempt, James Perry was arrested. In November, 2005, he was sentenced to 470 years in prison. This was not Perry's first crime. Police had been seeking him for five years. He had come to be known as "The Mall Rapist." The young woman's description of this man was crucial in his capture.

At that sentencing a young woman handled herself as Jesus would. The sentencing judge asked if she had anything to say to the man.

"Yes, I do," she said softly.

She approached the man.

"When you were telling me to shut up, I was praying. You could have me, but you couldn't stop me from praying." she testified to the man.

"Even though you hurt me and my family, I forgive you."

"Thank you...I'm sorry," the man responded between sobs.

After appearances on Oprah, Good Morning America, Montel Williams, and 20/20, it's safe to say that the young woman who had gone through a few "minutes from hell" had indeed been used by God in an extraordinary way that brought attention and glory to His power. She wasn't surprised because, as a little girl, she had prayed that God would use her in such a way that would draw attention to Him.

Maybe it wasn't the way she had planned or expected, but He had answered her prayer. For you can figure by now that the little heroine in this story was none other than Cassie Chivers.

Money Waters of Trust

It had been years since the Collison family had taken an extended vacation and the time seemed right. Over the winter months, Mike and Linda discussed where to take a summer break. Mike was pushing for Colorado, but Linda wasn't sure. Later, Linda felt that they should go to New York. Mike let go of his dream for a trip west and said, "God, wherever you want us to go is fine with me." Linda soon phoned Michael and Ann, friends from Long Island, New York, where the Collisons had previously lived for five years.

"Hi, it's Linda," she began.

"Well, how are you?" asked Ann.

"We're doing great! Hey, we're thinking of coming out and seeing you guys this summer."

"That would be wonderful," Ann replied. "Let's put it on the calendar."

With the family vacation now planned, the Collisons immediately began to put some money into a savings account for the trip. It would have to be a modest trip built around visiting friends and some very careful budgeting. After only a few months of saving, Mike and Linda got some challenging news. They discovered that their son, Ryan, had been diagnosed with a benign tumor in his upper jaw that needed to be removed. There was some concern as to whether or not the procedure would even be covered by their insurance.

The Collisons began to pray while continuing to save for a vacation. One thing was certain. If insurance didn't cover the bill, there would be no vacation. There was no way the numbers would work to make it possible to go anywhere. Later in the spring Linda called the insurance company. The news wasn't at all what she had hoped for.

"We're sorry, but your insurance will not cover Ryan's procedure," was the rather cold and detached answer she received.

Linda hung up the phone and wanted to cry. She told Mike the insurance company's decision and, for a while, they both felt so discouraged, questioning everything. Then one Sunday morning they received a totally unexpected and encouraging surprise. A woman in church slipped them some money.

"This is for your vacation," was all she said.

It was a well-timed blessing for the couple that had already written off any chance of heading to the "Big Apple" that summer.

Over the next few weeks Linda prayerfully made calls and gathered information in order to appeal the insurance company's decision. They waded through the best way to present their case, but they were not in agreement as to its outcome. Mike was confident that the insurance company would reconsider their case and cover it, while Linda was feeling very unsure. Mike's prayer was to have faith to trust the Lord regardless of the outcome of the appeal. Along with friends and family that's the way they continued to pray.

The Collisons decided to set up two scenarios for a vacation. The first would be a one-week trip to Michigan to visit family. The second would also include a week in New York. They wanted the latter, but they kept their options open. During a conversation with a family friend, Jennifer in New York, they mentioned the insurance struggles they were going through.

"Do you think you guys are supposed to come to New York regardless, by faith, and watch God provide along the way?" asked Jennifer.

"We're not sure," was their reply.

The insurance grievance committee couldn't hear the appeal until five days before their vacation departure. The meeting day arrived, and Mike was feeling confidant.

"Honey, I think they're going to cover it!" was his hunch.

Mike was out biking when Linda called.

"They rejected it!"

"Say that again."

"They rejected us," repeated Linda.

The Collisons made a difficult call to New York to tell friends that they would not be making the trip. They began to pack for the trip to

Michigan. The car needed a new set of tires and they needed travel money, so Mike withdrew $450 from the vacation-turned-surgery savings account. The breakdown was $250 for travel and $200 for tires. One hour before they departed for Michigan the phone rang. It was Ann from New York.

"Hey, you guys, Michael and I have a strong sense that you are supposed to come out and see us," she began. "We believe God is going to provide for Ryan's surgery." Then there was more. "We want to give you $500 to help with your expenses."

Mike and Linda vacillated between feelings of gratitude and uncertainty. Was this a "God thing" or a "human thing?" They needed a little more time to process the humbling offer that had just been made to them. They told Ann they would call them from the road. Accepting the offer would require real humility. They prayed. Then they made a call.

"We're coming!"

The trip to New York would come via Michigan. While back "home" Mike helped his dad roof the chicken coop and he also did some work for his uncle. Both jobs earned $250, the amount that had been taken out for travel. That was a blessing. Linda had spent a day visiting old friends. Just as she was leaving, a friend named Michael handed her a check.

"This is for Ryan's surgery. I have no children, and I've prayed about it," he told her.

It was for $200, the amount of the tires. The $200 was significant because Linda had been worrying specifically about this money from the day the tires were bought and put on the vehicle. Now as the Collisons headed for New York, they were beginning to believe Jennifer's words that God would provide along the way.

The 16-hour drive further tested their resolve as their daughter, Alyssa, came down with the flu. Barely into Ohio, parents first before travelers, the Collisons nearly turned back after seeing her cramped and crying in the back seat. However, with Motrin and prayer they continued on their journey to New York.

Michael and Ann greeted the family warmly upon arrival. There were lots of hugs and a check for $500, just as they had promised.

"We want to give back whatever we don't use," Linda and Mike said in unison, feeling humbled yet again.

"Just consider it a gift from God," they declared.

The families spent a few days getting caught up on sleep and news and simply relaxing. On Thursday they planned to go to the beach, but rain kept them home. Friday brought hot and humid temperatures. The only debate was whether to go to the ocean beach or the bay beach. The group was divided fifty-fifty. Finally it was decided to go to the bay to avoid possible riptides.

Everyone planted chairs and coolers in the sand; toys came spilling out of their container; it was proving to be a great day. The kids loved the warm, shallow waters of the bay. As one who generally avoids the sun, it wasn't long before Mike was moaning and complaining.

"When can we go?" he asked.

Ann echoed the same sentiments, but the kids were having such a good time, so they were told to "zip it!"

Mike decided to distract himself by digging a large crater at the water's edge with the kids. Most of the nine gathered around and helped with scooping and dumping in water. Alyssa was sitting and splashing in the shallow water about eight feet off shore when she felt something odd on the sandy floor. She reached down and pulled it out of the water.

"Daddy, look what I found!"

It was a money clip with soggy money in it. Mike dried it off on a beach towel and put it in the diaper bag. They finished the day giddy with possibilities.

In the car, on the way back to their friend's home, Mike pulled the money out of the bag. The first bill he peeled from the money clip was a hundred! The next was the same! They continued removing bill after bill. With each one Mike and Linda looked at each other in utter amazement. Soon they had counted all the money that the clip held.

There was $1,496! The Collisons needed $1,450 to cover the balance of Ryan's surgery!

The Story of the Story

When the Collison got home their expense sheet showed there had been an extra $75 in gas receipts and $125 for the house sitter. But, in the mail, dated a week earlier, a check came for $200 attached to Logan's birthday card.

An addendum to the story reveals that in the mail waiting for them when they got home was a note from a friend in Colorado, where Mike had wanted to go initially.

Dear Mike,
This has been the worst summer I've ever seen in Colorado. Record heat and drought, fires everywhere, and the lakes and beautiful streams are either dried up or down to a trickle. It's been awful!

You picked a great summer NOT to come to Colorado for a vacation!
Best wishes,
Steve

The Starrs of Rawhide

John and Jan Gillespie had a vision to start a ranch for delinquent boys. They heard that Bart and Cherry Starr had the same vision. Jan had a really radical thought.

"Why don't you call Bart?" she asked her husband.

This was August of 1966. Bart was the quarterback of the world champion Green Bay Packers. This man was incredibly popular. Needless to say, John was definitely skeptical, but wanted to be polite while telling his wife she was crazy to even suggest such a thing.

"Honey, getting a hold of the Pope would be easier. Besides, he'll have an unlisted number," he said totally discounting the idea.

"How do you know?" countered Jan.

"Trust me, I know."

Two weeks went by as John tried to get in touch with Bart through various other contacts. In the meanwhile, a piece of property came up for sale that John felt would be ideal for the ranch. There were offers on it, but the owner really wanted to see it become a boys ranch.

John prayerfully put $2,500 down on the property. The money was borrowed from Jan's father and a businessman by the name of Paul Patz. Keep in mind it was 1966. That was a lot of money. Mrs. Gillespie persistently provoked her husband to try to call Starr. Being a typical "guy," John decided to show Jan just how goofy her idea was.

"Okay, I'll show you just how impossible this is going to be."

He called information and, amazingly, got Bart Starr's phone number!

"Jan, even if I get a hold of him, he'll probably be too busy to meet with us."

"John, just call him," she insisted. John dialed and a man answered.

"Hello."

"Is this the Starr residence?"

"Yes, it is."

"Is Mr. Starr there?"

"There is no Mr. Starr here, but Bart is."

"That's who I'd like to speak with."

"You're speaking to him."

After practically falling off his chair contemplating how he was going to explain this to his wife, John nervously proceeded.

"My name is John Gillespie. My wife and I have a desire to start a boys ranch. We heard you and Cherry might have the same interest. Is that true?"

"Yes, it is," Bart confirmed.

"Is it possible for us to get together and discuss this?" asked a now believing John.

"Sure."

"How do I make an appointment?"

"Well, you just have to ask for one."

"Uh, okay. I'd like to make an appointment."

"Great! Do you want to come over right now?" asked the future NFL Hall-of-Fame quarterback.

Within the hour the Gillespies and the Starrs were having supper. John had a presentation, complete with flip charts. The Starrs were impressed and agreed to help John raise capital for the venture.

A few months later, in November, a crisis situation arose. The banker called John and reminded him that if they didn't come up with $20,000 by Monday at 5 p.m., they would lose their down payment and the property would go back on the market. John contacted Bart who approached Vince Lombardi, coach of the Packers at the time, and asked him if he could speak to the players at practice about attending a luncheon in support of the boys ranch. Lombardi agreed to his request.

After briefly sharing the vision for the ranch the Packer "family" responded. In attendance that day were Packer greats, Jerry Kramer, Fuzzy Thurston, the late Henry Jordan and Elijah Pitts. Receivers Boyd Dowler and Carroll Dale were there along with Zeke Bratkowski. Each player had also brought along a local business leader or two to the luncheon.

"So, gentlemen, if you feel this is a worthy cause, I'd like to ask you to contribute. Thank you," finished Starr.

As the players and their guests exited, they handed Bart checks. One businessman waited until last and asked Bart if he would add up the amount. It came to $14,000. Without hesitation he wrote a check for the remaining $6,000! That man was a local contractor by the name of Julius "J.O." Johnson.

The ranch was built. Today, Rawhide Boys Ranch has become one of the leading juvenile rehabilitation programs in the nation, thanks in part to Bart and Cherry and the faith of Jan Gillespie, who believed her husband should call and God would work out the details.

By the way, two of the first boys to come to the Rawhide Boys Ranch were Jeff and John. And, yes, they had ties to the Packers. Their last names may sound familiar. They were related to the man after whom legendary Green Bay Packer Stadium is named. Jeff and John were grandsons of Packer Founder Curly Lambeau!

The Story of the Story

There is definitely a pleasant irony in this story proving that we never know whose lives we will be impacting when we reach out to help others.

A Fine Time to Leave Me, Loose Wheel

Dan and Mary Konkle loved their dependable, tan, 1982 Pontiac Le Mans. It ran like a top. During the summer of 1984 they got a flat tire, but that was no problem for Mr. Fix it to handle. Dan grabbed the spare, changed the flat and "old faithful" was back on the road again.

The next day while cruising in downtown traffic, Dan had a close call. A careless driver pulled in front of him. In order to avoid hitting the car, Dan swerved sharply to the right. In doing so he hit the curb with quite a bit of force. Other than the jolt to his system, and absorbing the curb, everything seemed to be all right. At least he thought so.

The following day Mary went to run some errands. She took along eleven-month-old son Jared. It was the usual congestion of 5 o'clock traffic. She drove down Racine Street and put on her directional in preparation to take a left turn. The light was still green as she turned the steering wheel. Suddenly, the car's steering wheel began to wobble uncontrollably. The force of it really hurt her arms as she tried to maintain control. She steered the car off the main part of the road and parked it near the curb.

"I must have another flat tire," was all she could imagine had happened. Mary quickly got out with Jared and walked around the back of the car to the sidewalk.

A car that had been following Mary pulled up behind the wounded Le Mans and parked. A frantic woman in her thirties, with short brown hair, exited her vehicle as if it were on fire. She bolted toward Mary.

"Oh, my God! Oh, my God! Are you all right?" she questioned hysterically, her hands on the cheeks of her ghostly white face.

"What's the matter?" asked Mary, who was mystified about all the panic and commotion.

"Your tire! Your tire!" she continued frantically.

"What do you mean? What are you talking about?" asked a peculiarly calm Mary.

"No, your tire, your tire!" she continued.

"I'm fine, really I am," assured Mary.

The woman settled down, took a deep breath, and then proceeded to describe to Mary what she had witnessed while driving behind her. Mary listened to what the woman had to say. Frankly, thirty seconds into the conversation, Mary came to the conclusion that the woman may have been at the local tavern a little too long. What she had said made no sense to Mary whatsoever.

"The tire is fine," said Mary. "But the steering wheel did wobble horribly as I turned the corner," she confessed to the still shaken woman.

Mary expressed concern to the lady that she did not want to drive the car because of the steering problem. If it had been just her she might have considered it, but she had her precious baby with her. She looked at the front tire one more time, and from what she had seen, there seemed to be nothing wrong with it.

"Can I give you a ride home?" said the now-somewhat-composed other driver.

"Oh, that would be so kind of you," Mary told her, accepting the offer.

When Mary got home she recounted the whole story to Dan. They loaded the kids into their other car, grabbed another tire, just in case they needed it, and off they went. On the way, Mary couldn't help but chuckle as she told Dan about the "crazy woman" and what she had told her. Dan had a good laugh right along with Mary.

Soon they were at the corner of 9th and Racine Streets. Thankfully, their car was still there, too. Dan approached the vehicle and, as Mary had said, the tire was not flat. However, it didn't take Dan long to realize that something was terribly wrong. He knelt down and leaned close to the tire and rim, and took a long, hard look.

Upon closer inspection, Dan could see the rim of the tire had cracked through completely, but it had broken in a perfect circle, just to the outside of each of the lug nuts. The only thing that was attached to the tire was the very center of the broken rim. In other words, the wheel had become totally separated from the car! The tire was, however, still sitting perfectly flush on the rim. If it had not been, it would have caved in or out, depending on how it was sitting on the rim. Mary and Dan looked at one another in silence for a few moments. Each had a confession to make to the other.

"Maybe the woman was right, honey," said Dan, echoing what Mary was thinking, but hadn't spoken aloud.

"Yeah, maybe so," added a humbled, repentant Mary, as they both gawked in amazement and gratitude at the tire and rim.

For the evidence now showed what the frantic woman had tried to tell Mary all along. She emphatically insisted that as she followed Mary around the corner she had seen the front right tire come off the car, roll toward the curb—and then come back onto the car!

For the Love of Trudi

In a split second a family's life can be changed forever. Such was the case shortly after midnight on Saturday July 9, 1994. Just hours earlier Trudi Marie Jeschke, 21, had decided to pass on an opportunity to join her sister's family and her father, Tom Jeschke, for a camping trip back home to Upper Michigan.

Trudi was living with her sister and brother-in-law, Trisha and Rob Hummel and their two children, Robert and Caitlyn. She had come to Appleton from her home in Michigan to find work and save money for school in the fall. Trisha was proud of Trudi's efforts to plan for her future, and wanted to help her do that by offering her a small but ample bedroom in the downstairs of their home.

On the afternoon of Friday, July 8, Trisha asked Trudi if she'd like to go home to Michigan with them to camp out, challenge the great outdoors and get in a little visiting with Mom who still lived in Upper Michigan.

"Aw c'mon, Trudi, come with us," pleaded her big sister.

"No, I think I'm going to hang out with some of the girls from my new job and get to know them a little better. I was just home last weekend anyway," she said.

Trisha knew when Trudi made up her mind on an issue it was fairly useless to argue the point further. So she didn't push it. The Hummels packed up the vehicle and headed out for the U.P. late in the afternoon of July 8th. They arrived at the campsite around suppertime. In the meantime, Trudi did go out that night with her friends. Later that evening, curled up on Trisha's and Rob's bed, Trudi placed a call to her boyfriend, Brad, who was stationed at an Air Force base in Montana. It was approximately 10 p.m.

Brad and Trudi were still visiting on the phone over an hour later when a man broke into the house. Trudi, realizing she was in trouble, screamed and began shouting out her address to Brad. The intruder, startled to come upon the young woman screaming out her address, aimed his gun and shot her point blank in the chest.

It wasn't until the early morning hours of July 9th that the Appleton Police Department had made the call to Upper Michigan that notified the Hummels and other family members that Trudi had been murdered. They requested that the immediate family come to the Appleton police station at around 10 o'clock that morning. Arriving in various vehicles and at different times were Tom Jeschke, Trisha and Rob, Linda Jeschke, and the Gradys, a couple who were the in-laws of Tom's friend, Avery. The Gradys, though not family, came to give Tom support.

Trapped beneath a mountain of grief and living with a hole in her heart that seemed too deep to ever heal, Trisha had so many questions.

"Why was Trudi murdered? Shouldn't it have been me in that bed? How will we live without her? Can we ever go back to that home again?"

The last question, voiced aloud, received a unanimous "No!" from Trisha's mom Linda, her twin sisters, Terri and Traci and her dad. Rob and Trisha would not return to the place where this horror had occurred.

At this point Don and Carol, who had accompanied Tom to the police station, made an unbelievably gracious offer to the Hummel family.

"Would you like to come and stay with us until you can get back on your feet and decide what comes next for your family?"

"Yes, that's so kind of you," they both accepted gratefully though they were a little surprised at the strangers' generosity.

Don and Carol provided the Hummels a place of their own in the upstairs of the home where they could just "be." Trisha was relieved that, given the state she was in, she wouldn't have to chase her nearly two-year-old and five year-old around protecting the Grady's home from little ones.

As the days progressed, Carol would gently and compassionately ask Trisha how she was doing.

"I'm okay," Trisha would respond. Trisha was cautious about opening her heart and expounding on the enormity of the pain she was feeling.

Carol understood that Trisha was experiencing a tremendously difficult time. One evening, a few weeks into the Hummel's stay, Carol decided to share an experience from her past with Trisha that she hoped would demonstrate that she truly understood their pain. Perhaps it would bring a measure of hope to Trisha and her family. They were in the living room together when Carol asked a question.

"Trisha, do you mind if I share my story with you?" she asked.

No, not at all," said Trisha as she leaned forward to listen more closely.

"One night, when I was 16, a man broke into the house where I was babysitting. He was actually in the process of raping me when my uncle arrived back home," she said. "The intruder shot my uncle and then escaped. Our lives were changed forever."

Trisha was moved that this woman would care enough about her to share such a deeply personal tragedy with her.

"It has taken me years to be able to talk about it," explained Carol. "As a matter of fact, very few people even know it happened, but God has given me healing over the years. I know, Trisha, that He will do the same for you. Someday 'your story' may be able to help others," she told the grieving young woman.

As several weeks passed, Rob and Trisha began to look for a new home. The old one hadn't sold, but it was time to make the effort to establish a "new normal." Their search took them to Greenville, at the time a tiny rural community, where they found a ranch home and wonderful neighbors. Although it felt like a violation to Trudi's memory to move on, they did, knowing that Trudi would have wanted them to embrace life again.

Appleton detectives continued to follow any and all leads that might solve the case to find the monster that had committed this murder. Almost eight months after the shooting, detectives Dan Woodkey and Randy Cook called Trisha in the early evening with some news.

"You aren't going to believe this, but we think we got him," they announced.

They gave some horrific details of this man's past and how he'd spent serious time in jail for a variety of heinous crimes, but one particular crime they referred to caused Trisha to nearly drop the phone!

Not long after his arrest for two other murders the man confessed to also killing Trudi Marie Jeschke. This was shocking in itself, but it was the crime that he'd committed 30 years earlier that prompted the Jeschkes and the Hummels to recognize that God, even in the midst of grief and confusion, had been watching over them and taking care of even the smallest details of their lives. Was this simply a coincidence? Not a chance. The odds of what had been revealed to them were unbelievable.

You see, the man who killed Trudi Jeschke was David Spanbauer. Though this would be his last crime, his laundry list of evil included many more crimes, including a rape and attempted murder committed back in 1960. His first victim was none other than Carol Larson (Grady), the incredible woman who, along with her husband, Don, had brought such hope and comfort to the Hummels over that six-week period in 1994!

The Story of the Story

What are the odds of these families being brought together through tragedy, much less tragedies perpetrated by the same man? Trisha Hummel offered this story, and Carol Grady thought it would help someone as well. We pray it does.

For the Record

"Dan, that's the song!" hollered Joyce Longsine as she flung dish-water all over the kitchen.

Soon Dan was dancing in the living room in celebration. If the Longsines were not people of faith who didn't believe in "Godincidences," Dan, for one, could easily have been on the verge of a heart attack after seeing what he was about to see.

It was the spring of 1982. Dan Longsine was working the 2 to 10 p.m. shift when a catchy song came on WEMI Radio. He thought he heard the announcer say that the title was *They're Holding Up the Ladder*. Ever have a tune that you just can't get out of your mind? Well, that was the case with Dan. It was so much so that when he got home from work he told his wife Joyce about it.

"Honey, I heard a great song on the radio tonight. I want to see if we can find it tomorrow," he said.

"What's the name of it?" asked his wife.

"I thought the DJ said something like, *They're Holding Up the Ladder*, but I'm not sure," he confessed. Dan plays guitar so he was anxious to find it, get the lyrics and possibly learn to play it.

The next day Dan and Joyce left directly after lunch, leaving dirty dishes in the sink, to go music shopping. It was a beautiful day for the 20-minute trek that landed them at the Evangel Bookstore where they believed they could find what they were looking for. It was there they ran into Rick Regenfuss, a childhood friend of Dan's who happened to be behind the counter.

"Rick, I'm looking for a song," said Dan. "I think it's called *They're Holding Up the Ladder*."

"Who sings it?" asked Rick.

"I don't know," was all the Longsines could offer.

"Do you know what label it's on?"

"I have no clue," acknowledged Dan, realizing the search was not going to be as easy as he had hoped.

"Hmmm," sighed Rick. "I don't know that we have a song by that title here," he said as he searched the new music 45s and albums.

Rick couldn't find the title in anything he had to offer. The Longsines merely saw this as a stumbling block not realizing that this response would become a pattern over the next few hours. Although disappointed, the couple held out hope that they would find what they were looking for at a different store.

Off they went to another store not far away called The Exclusive Company. It was known for the huge library of songs it carried, containing literally hundreds of titles. They figured if anybody had it, the Exclusive Company did. Unfortunately, they heard the same questions.

"Who does the song? What label is it on?"

"We have no idea," was all the couple could echo for the second time in an hour.

Now the search extended to yet another music store. Soon they arrived at Lighthouse Books. The woman working there was kind and accommodating, but the results were the same. The Longsines and the woman spent a great deal of time combing through the records like "blind squirrels hoping to stumble upon a nut," but to no avail. Dan and Joyce graciously thanked the woman for her help, resigned to the fact that this day was not going to fulfill their quest.

It was late afternoon when Dan and Joyce headed back to report to Rick at Evangel Bookstore that their mission, at least for today, would be a failure. They had purposed, however, that they would not go home completely empty handed. They did spot an album from a group they liked, the "Florida Boys." Their latest album was entitled *Treasures*. Dan looked at the songs on the album and was satisfied to take it home as consolation.

So off to the counter they went to pay for it. Rick felt badly he had not been able to help them. He knew how determined the Longsines had been to find their song and he offered some encouragement.

"I'm sorry, guys. I'll keep my eyes and ears open for *They're Holding Up the Ladder*," he comforted.

"Thanks," was all the Longsines could muster as they made their way out of the store.

When they arrived home Joyce began to wash the neglected lunch dishes still sitting in the sink. Meanwhile, Dan peeled the cellophane from the new album. He pulled the record from its jacket cover. He never even bothered to see what songs were listed on the label. He gently placed it on the turntable, set the needle down on it and walked away. The first song began to play.

It was then that soapy water flew from Joyce's hands as Dan yelped in amazement while dancing on the living room floor. The song playing was none other than *They're Holding Up the Ladder*!

If the Florida Boys had indeed recorded the song they were listening to, why hadn't they read so on the back of the album cover when they were at the store?

Dan walked over to the turntable, lifted the needle, and pulled the record album to his eyes. He was stunned to find that the album was not, in fact, that of the "Florida Boys," but of a group called the "Inspirations"—the group that had actually recorded the song—the same one Dan had heard last night on WEMI Radio!

The Story of the Story

When we heard this one we knew that it would challenge the mystery minds of many of our readers. Upon some investigation we discovered that the "Florida Boys" and the "Inspirations" recorded on the same label. Is it possible that someone showed up for work a little tired and mixed up the albums and their covers on an assembly line in Nashville? Your guess is as good as ours. And, oh, Dan still has the album and the cover, too!

Elizabeth's Got Your Number

Pat and Wayne Sorenson had a weekly Friday night routine that included going out for fish and spending time together. One particular Friday night in April of 1999 the routine was altered. Wayne had gone out of town to compete in a handball tournament. This left Pat free to make other plans.

She called her hairdresser that morning and made an appointment for a haircut. It was cancelled later that afternoon. She called a good friend to see if they could meet for fish that evening. Her friend agreed, but then called later to say she was ill and couldn't make it. At the last minute Pat called Jan Burnside, a friend she hadn't seen in over a year. They went out for fish and then back to Jan's home to chat and get caught up on each other's news and family events.

They were there for only a short time when the phone rang.

"Hello," answered Jan.

"Can you help me?" said the woman with slurred speech.

Jan struggled to understand what the woman was saying. It became apparent that there was a health-related issue happening on the other end of the line. In just a matter of minutes they identified the caller as Elizabeth Austin, a 90-year-old woman who lived with her schnoodle, Ollie. Jan immediately hung up and alerted Pat of the need to find out what was wrong. They went over to Elizabeth's home.

When they arrived at Elizabeth's, they found her suffering from the immediate effects of a stroke. Jan called 9-1-1. Within minutes, the paramedics arrived, assessed the situation and then transported Elizabeth to the hospital. Her nephew, Vern, came over to the house and was going to take Ollie to the kennel for the night. Jan felt concerned for the poor animal that had already been exposed to the confusion and trauma of the recent events.

"Would you mind if I took him home?" asked Pat. "He has been through so much tonight," she finished.

"Sure, I can't see why not," said Vern.

Pat scooped up Ollie and took him home with her for the night.

Elizabeth survived the stroke and, upon release from the hospital, was sent to a nursing home to convalesce. She was also reunited with Ollie.

Pat and Jan visited Elizabeth often during her stay in the hospital, as well as in the nursing home. Eventually, Elizabeth went to live full time in an assisted living home. They continued to visit her there, as well. Ollie would live with Pat and Wayne for the next three years, but was a regular visitor with Pat to see Elizabeth.

During the time they visited Elizabeth, Pat and Jan got a chance to renew their own friendship while also developing a wonderful friendship with Elizabeth.

There are several things worth noting about the unusual sequence of events on that Friday night. That evening found the elderly woman in dire circumstances. Elizabeth's intention was to phone her neighbor, but she had misdialed the very last digit, calling Jan instead. Thanks to caller ID, Jan and Pat were able to look up Elizabeth Austin's name and number in the phone book and, ultimately, go to her rescue. Until that night, Pat and Jan did not even know Elizabeth Austin!

Thorn in the Hand of a Fool

Lenny Wilcox was a bit hesitant about telling people he was pursuing a new found faith. He knew that one person in particular who would give him a hard time about this was his father. His dad had a problem with alcohol. It was no secret to anyone who knew him, but, like most who struggle with alcoholism, he would be one of the last to know. Mr. Wilcox could be quite belligerent at times while under the influence. He fancied himself a freethinker and, as such, had a wisecrack for any given scenario.

One day the elder Wilcox, who had been drinking, dropped by to see his son. It was becoming a "sport" to give his son a hard time about his faith. Lenny's dad sat across the table preparing to sarcastically recite verses from the Bible to him in an effort to make fun of his son and of God. In the middle of the table stood a vase of roses. Mr. Wilcox reached into the bouquet and grabbed one of the beautiful flowers. He rolled it around in his hand and pounded the table surface with it to help make his point. Meanwhile Lenny was praying to himself.

"Dear God, give me the right words to say to my father," was his unspoken prayer as he parted his Bible open on the table.

Lenny's dad dealt out one verbal jab after another. Lenny sat in silence, waiting for God to speak to him, and possibly through him, to his father. Midway of the third remark his dad let out a holler.

"Owww!" he yelled. He had carelessly embedded a thorn from the rose into the thumb of his hand.

At that precise moment a beleaguered Lenny looked down into his Bible. It had fallen open to the book of Proverbs. His eyes fell on Proverbs 26:9. He read it aloud to his father. Lenny's dad sobered immediately and gave his son a look that suggested he had seen a ghost. The man now sat at the table with reverence, awe and humility. The verse froze his tongue into silence.

Sadly, it was no real surprise that the next day Lenny's dad was back in the tavern. He was pushing in the coin release on the pool table when he let out another scream. A sharp pain reminded him that the thorn was still in his hand. At that precise moment the drunk looked up at the TV anchored to the wall over the bar to see a Christian program on the screen! He tried to drown out the conviction that he may possibly be on the receiving end of a message from the Almighty with yet another drink.

Lenny's experience with his father from the day before had certainly encouraged and even deepened his faith, even if it had not done so for his father. Lenny was grateful God could be trusted to defend him as He had proven at the table with his father.

So what did the Bible verse in Proverbs 26:9 have to say? Lenny was able to speak truth in the exact moment that his inebriated father was not only carelessly mocking God's word, but as the sharp thorn embedded into his dad's thumb.

Lenny had read aloud to his father, *"As a thorn goeth up into the hand of a drunkard, so is a parable in the mouth of fools!"*

Hope at the Bottom of the Pool

It had become somewhat of a tradition for the Tom and Denise Griesbach clan to get away to ease the strain and bustle of the holiday season. On December 21, 1996, that looked like going away with four other couples for a stay at the Best Western in Shawano. Tom and Denise took their six kids and with all included there would be 19 kids and five sets of parents. That's enough for a good party and lots of excitement. Little could anyone have known just how much excitement would be right around the corner.

Upon arrival, bags were unpacked and swimming suits were brought out. In short time some were in the hot tub while the rest began to splash in the pool. Tom was in the hot tub when he asked Kime Biggar if she would watch little Tatiana who was only three years old. No one noticed, but Tatiana had followed Dad out of the hot tub. Kime thought Tom was aware of that fact, and seemed perplexed that Tom wanted her to keep an eye on Tatiana who was following Dad. Trouble was, Tatiana took a detour that neither Tom nor Kime had seen. She headed for the pool.

With no life jacket on, fearless little Tatiana decided to go for a swim. Thank goodness Wanda Winterfeldt happened to be walking by the pool on the way to her room when she spotted someone on the bottom of the pool. At first she thought it was one of the older kids swimming around down there, but she soon realized that whoever it was wasn't moving! To this day there is some mystery as to how Wanda cleared the railing due to its height and other circumstances, but she did. Fully clothed she dove into the pool.

Within seconds she grabbed the child who had been face down at the bottom and pulled her to the surface. It was only then that Wanda realized it was little Tatiana. The child was blue, limp and not breathing. Wanda laid her down on her side. Tatiana began to sputter and cough out some water and eventually started to cry. Just then Wanda's husband,

Wes, arrived on the scene and grabbed the tiny child. Then Tom arrived.

"Tatiana, cough!" yelled Tom.

She did and the water began to pour out of her. Suddenly, Mom was there in the thick of it all also.

Within a few minutes normal color began to come back to Tatiana. There was a startling realization of what had just happened and, miraculously, had not happened. The amount of tears shed could have filled the pool. The Griesbachs had said goodbye to Jesse Joe who died at the age of seven on May 9, 1995. He had cerebral palsy and died suddenly from reflux. Now they had just seen their Tatiana literally pulled back from the other side.

Tom and Denise packed little Tatiana into the car intent on getting to Theda Clark Medical Center in Neenah to see Tatiana's doctor, John Swanson, who happened to be on call that afternoon. Chest and blood work were done as a safety measure, and to reassure Mom and Dad that everything was indeed okay.

No sooner had they arrived back at the hotel than Tatiana announced her intentions. Can you guess what she wanted to do? You got it, go swimming! Talk about no fear? Tatiana's life had been spared, but what was she thinking wanting to go back to what easily could have been her watery grave?

The possible answer to this question may have been revealed when on January 6, 1997, just a few weeks after the fateful event, Denise and Tatiana were making beds at the "Griesbach hotel." It was then that little Tatiana had an interesting question for Mom.

"Mom, why would you be sad if I died when I fell in the water?" she asked.

"Well, honey, because we would miss you."

"Mom, Jesse wants to play with me in heaven," were her next words.

By this time Mom sensed that something was up and that Tatiana was having a flashback to December 21. Longing not to miss the moment, Denise carefully asked Tatiana a question.

"Did Jesse say anything to you?"

"No," she replied matter of factly.

What came next was nothing short of astounding!

"Mom, I saw Jesus."

"You saw Jesse?" asked Denise, wondering if she had not heard her correctly.

"No, I saw Jesus," she replied calmly. "He was wearing a white shirt and he was glowing," said Tatiana. "I reached out to touch him, but before I could, the water splashed me and Wanda picked me up."

The Story of the Story

Denise Griesbach said that as her toddler waddled away she wanted to grab her and never let her go. Her prayer was that it would be a long time before this little girl would be playing with Jesse Joe. Tatiana's words on this cold January day did confirm just how near she really had come to "going home." Needless to say, December 25, 1996 was a special Christmas with nothing being taken for granted at the Griesbachs. Santa didn't need to leave a thing. God had already left His gift behind on December 21.

A Father's Prayer

It was February 2, 1999. Marc Lutz and his buddy Dave, two of the most promising 19-year-old guys on the University of Wisconsin-Oshkosh campus, were looking around the lecture hall for a place to sit where they could stretch out their legs. They spotted two such openings in the middle of the center section so they made their way there. They figured there would be about 200 students in this particular chemistry class. Making her way into the class was a 19-year-old blonde who sat directly in front of Marc and Dave in one of the three seats available. She definitely caught the guys' eyes.

"Man, she's hot!" Marc blurted under his breath. Dave heard him and agreed.

Eventually, the young woman took the first step and introduced herself to Marc and Dave after laughing at how funny they were. Dave immediately really liked this attractive young woman. Marc thought she was gorgeous, but he was in a relationship already, so he gave way to his friend, kind of. The young woman went home that same afternoon and had a talk with her mom.

"Mom, today I think I met the man I'm going to marry!"

"Really? That's wonderful!" said her mother, knowing to not say any more than that for now.

As time went on Marc realized that with every opportunity to be around this woman she was capturing his heart a little more. In retrospect, being a "typical" guy, he failed to see that she was sending signals to him, too.

Before long, Marc found himself talking to his mom, Lois, about her. He even shared some of his insecurities about the whole situation.

"Mom, you don't know who she is. She could never be interested in me," he confessed somewhat anxiously.

"Marc, she doesn't know who you are!" said Lois, spoken like a true mom. Lois listened as he went on to tell how pretty she was and that he did really want to ask her out.

A few weeks after the last day of their class, Marc found himself in a phone booth in downtown Oshkosh fumbling through his pocket for some change. After three or four attempts at calling listings of people with her last name, he struck gold.

"Hi…it's Marc from class…how are you?" he asked.

"I'm good, how are you?" she said enthusiastically.

They chatted for about 15 minutes. After hanging up, they both felt that friendship with one another would be an important first step. By this time Amanda's schedule had gotten incredibly busy. Still, she made it clear that she wanted to pursue a relationship with Marc. They began to see one another whenever possible, and "sparks" were definitely flying.

On October 6, 2004, Steve had a business meeting in Neenah with Marc's dad, Vic Lutz.

"Steve, I'm familiar with who you are. Lois and I used to watch your *Leap of Faith* TV program on FOX-11 in Green Bay."

The show ran on Sunday mornings from 1998 to 1999. We interviewed guests about their faith and usually had a singer on as well. Vic then posed a question.

"Do you remember when you interviewed a woman by the name of Amanda Streblow?"

"Oh, sure, she was Miss Oshkosh. I'll never forget that—she was a wonderful down-to-earth young woman. She was a great guest, a young woman of faith who was using her platform to be a role model for young women, not to mention she was beautiful," I recalled.

"Yes, she was. I have to tell you, Steve, that I was so impressed with that young woman that, after the program, I prayed to God that He would give my son a woman just like her."

That particular program ran on June 26, 1999. It was the first week in July when Marc finally had his first "real" date with this very special girl from school. Marc came home one day shortly after that and had what he thought would be first-time news, but it apparently was not a total surprise.

"Dad, I have to tell you, I had a date with a beautiful girl the other day. Her name is Amanda," to which Vic replied, "Yeah, and her last name is Streblow!"

The Story of the Story

The 1999 timeline for this story is just incredible. Marc and Amanda met February 2 and instantly became friends. Amanda was named Miss Oshkosh on March 6. It was after that when Marc really felt like the odds would be against him. Marc and Amanda began a serious friendship in May. The TV show with Amanda's appearance ran June 26. They began dating the first week in July. And the father's prayer was answered on June 1, 2002. That's the day Marc Lutz and Amanda Streblow were married!

An Open Door

Rich and Linnea Forney had moved in with Linnea's mom and dad, Don and Vicky Karl. Some modifications had been made to the basement to accommodate them, which included heat and smoke activated fire detectors. Linnea's childhood bedroom would now become hers and Rich's. It had a few quirks, including the fact there were no windows to the outside, but one of the most annoying was a door that wouldn't close. It took a really good "pull and yank" technique to get it to clear the carpet and close all the way.

Although their new living conditions weren't ideal, the Forneys were, nonetheless, grateful to have a place to stay, not only for themselves, but also for their two children, Chalisse, 4, and Cody, 2. Chalisse would sleep upstairs with her Aunt Brianna, 13, while a storage room near their bedroom was converted into a nursery for Cody. They put up a wall and door to separate his room from the rest of the basement and the wood burner.

On Friday, October 29, 1999, Linnea and Vicky left for a women's retreat, a well-deserved break for both of them. Rich, Don, Chalisse, Cody and Brianna remained at the homestead. On the morning of Sunday, the 31st, Rich had hastily gotten out of bed to get the children ready for church.

That afternoon Brianna and Chalisse decided to go four wheeling. Rich put Cody down for his nap and turned the monitors on upstairs. Don, meanwhile, was grading the driveway. Twenty minutes after Rich took Cody downstairs for his nap, the girls returned home crying. They had tipped over the four-wheeler that Brianna was driving and, though unharmed, both girls were a bit shaken. Rich thought it would be a good idea if Chalisse took a nap. Rich put her to bed and waited outside her door for her to fall asleep. Then he was going to go out and help Don with the landscaping.

Suddenly, Rich heard a faint ringing, like a timer going off. Rich was concerned that the noise would wake up Cody. Rich went down the half-flight of stairs to the kitchen. There was a haze in the air, and he wondered if perhaps the oven had been left on with a few pans left in it, but the oven was off. He looked around and then it hit him! The ringing was from one of the fire alarms downstairs!

Rich tore down another half-flight of stairs to the basement. A million thoughts went through his head. Was this why Cody had been so quiet for the last twenty minutes? Was he overcome with smoke? What was burning and why?

When he turned to enter the basement, he was hit with a wall of black smoke that filled half of the basement. There was a stench of chemicals or plastic burning. He buried his mouth in the crook of his arm the whole time feeling like his heart would explode. The ringing was getting louder!

Rich scrambled past their bedroom where a quick glance showed that there were flames coming off the bed in the middle of the room. They disappeared into the black cloud yet still, somehow, lit up the room like lighting in a thunderhead. Then it occurred to Rich what had happened. In his haste to get everyone up and going in the morning, he had left on the electric blanket! But, there was no time for regret at the moment.

Rich proceeded fearlessly down the hall to get Cody. Everything seemed to move in slow motion. Rich grabbed the doorknob to Cody's room and opened the door. His nightlight was shining next to his crib. He was motionless as he lay there wrapped in his blankets. There was a slight breeze in the room coming from the cracks around the door leading to the storage room that hadn't been sealed yet. Remarkably, there was no smoke in the room at all.

Rich scooped up Cody who immediately began to cry. As he tucked Cody as close to his body as he could, Rich also began to weep with gratitude. Rich secured Cody in his grasp and went back the same way that he had come. He could hear the fire crackling from their bedroom. The heat waves were intense. Rich turned his back to the door and made his way upstairs to safety. Soon firemen were on the scene and everything was under control. Thank God everyone was safe!

The Salvation Army put the Forneys up for the night. Rich had a very restless night, for all the obvious reasons, but there was one thing in particular that kept nagging him. It was something that a fireman had said before he left the scene that day. Rich just couldn't get it out of his mind. Rich decided he needed to do some investigating of his own.

The following day, November 1, Rich went back to the house and headed downstairs to make some observations of the burnt area. He went into their bedroom, the one he had gone past on his way to get Cody. He had seen flames coming from the bed and he had felt the heat. As he looked around, he noted that the door had been burned, peeled and significantly marred on the inside, right up to the doorframe. Everything in the room was charred, paper bags had been turned to ashes, CDs melted on the shelf, while the TV, phone and fan were simply left as piles of goo. This evidence strongly substantiated what the fireman had told him.

"It's a good thing that the bedroom door was shut. If it hadn't been, the whole house would have gone up in flames!" he had proclaimed confidently.

Before Rich went back upstairs he stared at the little unburnt strip of carpet from underneath the door where it had closed directly above it. This was just another fact confirming the fireman's claim that the door had indeed been closed during the fire. Because of that, the little nursery closest to the bedroom where the fire broke out was untouched, and so was precious Cody!

To this day, Rich has had a few questions that are still unanswered. He was certain that he had seen flames coming out of the bedroom as he was going to get Cody. He felt the intense heat that would not have been there if the door had been closed. So how could the door have gotten closed, especially with the "carpet flaw" that kept the door from ever closing?

Also, if the door to the bedroom had been closed, there would have been no smoke to set off the fire detector, which alerted him to go and get Cody. If the door had been open the fire would have spread like wildfire and certainly would have taken Cody with it.

What happened downstairs in the Karl's home on the afternoon of

October 31, 1999? No one really knows. What's important is that because the same door was apparently open and closed at the same time, a little boy is alive and a house was saved, and only heaven knows how that happened!

From the Mouth of a Babe

It's never pleasant to have car trouble, but it's a mother's night-mare to be stranded along the roadway with small children. Cheryl Edwards knew the feeling.

It was a pleasant spring day as she cruised with her three small children, Nikki 8, Paul 6, and Amanda 4, heading down the busy three-lane London Boulevard in Portsmouth, Virginia. Suddenly the old green Chevy broke down. Cheryl did manage to pull over to the far right lane, but she was still dangerously in the midst of traffic. This situation created more than the dilemma of questioning what could be wrong with the vehicle, but what now was the next course of action?

As she sat in the hushed vehicle, with traffic whizzing around them on the left, she made mental notes of her options. She didn't want to get out of the truck because of the danger of being hit, but she knew they could not just stay there either. A bit further down the road was a shopping center where she could go and phone for help, but she didn't feel at all good about leaving her children alone in the car. So what's she to do? She had an idea.

"We're going to pray for guidance," she told her children.

First mom prayed, then Nikki and Paul, each asking for divine intervention. They waited a few minutes, but there didn't appear to be any immediate answer.

"Okay, let's find a phone," said Cheryl who had now made a deci-sion to take the children and somehow safely leave the vehicle and pursue help. It was then that a tiny voice piped up.

"Mom, I haven't prayed yet!" said little Amanda.

"Oh, I'm sorry sweetheart, go ahead," she said realizing that this couldn't hurt.

"Dear God, please send someone to help us. Our truck is broke and we need to get out of here," came these words from the mouth of a babe.

As Cheryl lifted up her head she saw two incredibly large men walking toward their truck. She did not see where they had come from, but there was a Virginia Power Truck parked just up the way. Without saying a word the men pushed them off the road and out of traffic!

The Truth in the Tornado

In just seconds, a small town had been decimated by a weather phenomenon known as a tornado. It had been a peaceful evening, apparently the "calm before the storm." At 8:22 on Saturday, August 29, 1992, the lives of the people living in Wautoma exploded into the national news temporarily, but into local history forever.

As the dark, eerily yellowish sky produced the tornado, a man who had been driving on a rural highway was forced to stop alongside a debris-obstructed highway. He reported that his ears popped as he heard what sounded like a roaring freight train coming right toward him. The post-storm record would show that the tornado had cut a devastating swath 22-miles long, and one-mile wide, quite extraordinary even by former tornado statistics. When the dust had settled, tragically a couple people from Wautoma had lost their lives, but it was remarkable there were not more fatalities given the size and power of the storm.

Many tornados leave mysteries in their wake, and the one that hit the small town of Wautoma was no different. A woman named Pearl was found underneath a single wall from her home. Nothing else from her home could be found anywhere. A heavy toilet, from someone else's home, was found nearby. It had been tossed like a rag into the treacherous winds of doom. There was a report of one fortunate little girl who had a picture window land on her that shattered yet, miraculously, did not cut her!

One folktale told to this day of the Wautoma tornado is what had occurred at a restaurant called The 19th Hole. It seems that the powerful force of the wind took a plastic drinking straw and embedded it into the wall made of stone at the eatery while napkins on the bar close by were left unmoved!

Another peculiarity happened at the United Methodist Church just south of town. Pictures showed the church in total ruins. Nothing was left of the building or its contents, but the altar, barely visible in the rubble. More astonishing was the fact that the Bible still stood on its stand in its customary place on the altar. But what very well could be the most unusual remnant of the tornado's aftermath was the "silent sermon" that this particular Bible told.

The undamaged Bible was open to Psalm 77.

"The clouds poured out water, the skies sent out a sound; your arrows also flashed about. The voice of thunder was in the whirlwind; the lightnings lit up the world; the earth trembled and shook."

The Story of the Story

When we made our list of chapter ideas this story was on the list, but somehow it got buried underneath the heap until near the end of our writing. Our friend, Bob Gardinier, said that he had heard the story on a national radio broadcast. That was enough of a Godincidence to know that the story belonged here.

Bob arranged to have the transcript of the show sent to us, but yet we wanted some more details. Steve tried to contact someone that he knew from Wautoma, but he couldn't find his name in the phone book.

For some reason, Brady and Shelley Onsager, business associates of his, came to mind. He phoned them and within minutes Shelly, who had lived in Wautoma (but was not in the tornado), gave us needed details of the fateful day.

In a previous attempt to research the story on the Internet, Steve found the following:

HeirloomsLost.com
Message Board
Name: Kim Walters
Subject: photos—Wautoma Wis.
Date: Monday, May 19, 2003 at 11:46:04 pm
Searching for photos of the Ed Fisher family that may have blown away during the tornado of 1992 in Wautoma. If you found any photos in that area I am interested in seeing them. Thanks.

Nothing would be a warmer Godincidence to us than to have those pictures returned to her as a result of this story.

The Man Without a Face

Pastor Dick Balken walked up to the door of the small rural home. Sometimes as a pastor you have to deal with God's will, and at other times, the devil's. Sadly this night would be the latter. It was his appointed, unenviable job to tell Norb and Joyce Baumhardt the news that their youngest daughter, Paula, 20, had been murdered. It was yet another case of "love gone bad." Unable to cope with the latest breakup, ex-boyfriend Robert, 23, had made the decision that if he couldn't have Paula, no one would.

Norb knew the man-child who had dated his daughter had the capacity to kill. On one occasion, after learning that Robert had hit his daughter, Norb gave him a warning.

"If you touch her again, you'll have to deal with me," he warned sternly.

"I'll kill you!" snapped Robert right back at Norb and, in that moment, Norb knew he meant it.

"Then start with me," Norb said to the well-built bully who had steely, cold eyes.

Because of that threat, Paula avoided her own home and family after the breakup, fearful of what could happen. It wasn't unusual for Robert to bring Paula roses during good times and bad. But on March 21, 1985, he made one last delivery. Apparently, after Paula had told him that she would not be coming back to him, he bought one yellow rose and came looking for her.

Paula was babysitting out in the country when Robert showed up. No one's certain how he did it, but he lured her out of the home. When Paula realized what was about to happen she attempted to flee, but Robert shot her in the back right above the heart. She died instantly. Robert put a yellow rose on the step of the home, then took the same shotgun and blew the side of his face off with the first shell. He did not die. Determined to be with Paula, he succeeded on the second attempt.

About four days after Paula's funeral, Norb found himself sitting in his living room chair grieving the loss of his daughter. Suddenly a mist or fog developed in front of him. In the midst of the fog stood the image of Paula! She was smiling, her hands outstretched, palms up. Before Norb could speak to her, she vanished. He made the decision that if this, or something like it, ever happened again, he would speak to her and ask her questions before she slipped away.

In the days directly after the murder, Norb kept having visions of the face of the man with the cold, steely eyes who had murdered his little girl. He even blamed himself for what had happened. But what would haunt him most was the nagging question for which he had no answer.

"Is Paula in the same spiritual state as Robert?"

Then, just a few weeks after the tragedy, it happened again, but this time Norb was prepared. The fog developed while he was sitting in the living room. Before he knew it he was looking at what appeared to be a huge movie screen.

From the upper right hand corner were thousands of people in brown robes with hoods marching to the lower left hand corner of the "screen."

"What does this mean?" Norb asked aloud.

To this day he is not sure if it was actually an audible voice, but something or someone spoke to him as he asked his questions.

"These people are all marching to their judgment," came the answer.

"Is Paula among them?"

"No, these are all murderers from around the world who are going to their judgment," said the voice.

"Is Robert among them?" was Norb's next question.

"Yes, Robert's among them."

Norb looked for Robert in the crowd of thousands. Certainly he would be able to spot immediately the face of the cold-blooded man who had changed the heart of their family forever. As they moved closer, and he was able to see the robed figures more clearly, he noticed something about them.

"They have no faces," Norb said in amazement.

"That's right. They are faceless," confirmed the voice.

"I can't see Robert!" said Norb

"That's right. From this moment you never will. His face will be blotted from your memory forever," were the last words Norb heard before the screen went dark.

And from *that* moment and *still* to this day, Norbert Baumhardt has absolutely no memory or recollection of his daughter's murderer's face!

The Lost Wallet

Ron Mandich was standing in the Louisville Airport looking out a window when he saw a taxi parked in front of the terminal. It was not just any taxi, but "the" taxi. He had spent the previous 30 minutes going from taxi stand to taxi stand in an unsuccessful attempt to find this particular taxi.He dashed out of the airport toward the cab. No, he did not want to go anywhere in it. He had another intention entirely.

As he approached the taxi Ron recognized the driver through the passenger window. The driver was looking into his lap counting something. Ron knew exactly what it was. It was his $400! He opened the door and quickly tried to snatch the money out of the man's hands.

"What are you doing, man?" shouted the driver as he immediately put the money back into his pants pocket.

"You know what I'm doing," said Ron. "That's my money!"

After several heated exchanges, Ron heard a voice and looked behind him to see a uniformed female Airport Security guard.

"Can I be of assistance?" she asked.

"I don't know if you can or can't, but this man has my money and I want it back!" said Ron.

She calmly asked Ron his name and address. After some discussion, she suggested that perhaps the best course of action would be to get the Louisville Police involved.

"You wait here and I'll go get a policeman," she said.

"No, *you* wait here and *I'll* go," Ron insisted, convinced that the man would drive off if she left the scene.

How had this man wound up with Ron's money?

Just an hour earlier, Ron and a colleague had taken that very same cab to the airport from a sales call they had made together. Since his colleague's flight was about to leave and Ron had an hour to wait, Ron told him to make a "run for it" and he would take care of the fare.

After paying and tipping the driver, Ron received some change back. He then grabbed his briefcase, suitcase and overcoat, kicked the door shut and walked to the airport entrance. Upon entering the terminal, his hands full, he still clutched the change he had just received. Looking to put the money away, Ron quickly realized that he had left his wallet on the seat of the taxi! As one might imagine, a slight panic set in.

On the ride to the airport, Ron had taken note of the taxi number on the dashboard of the cab. He also noted the driver's jacket that was made of many small pieces of different colored leather. Knowing time was of the essence he immediately called the cab company to report his missing wallet. He gave the rep from the taxi company the taxi number and a description of the driver, including the unusual leather jacket. He was calling from a payphone and asked to be called back at that number. Twenty minutes passed and they still had not called so he called them again.

"This is Ron Mandich. Did you locate that taxi yet?" he asked.

"Yes, we did," said the man on the other end of the line, "and the driver says there's no wallet in his cab."

"Sir, with all due respect, I am sure that I left my wallet on the back seat of that cab."

His frustrations and explanations had fallen on deaf ears. Ron filed a report with both the Airport Security and the Louisville Police Office in the airport. They offered no help, hope or encouragement about getting his wallet or his money returned. That's when Ron began to search for "the" taxi at all of the various taxi stands hoping that the driver may have had another fare to the airport.

After that unsuccessful endeavor, he dejectedly made his way back into the terminal. Ron vividly remembers standing in front of the large airport window with one foot on the radiator, his elbow on his knee and his hand holding his forehead while he talked to God about the whole mess. It was nothing short of a miracle then, an hour after he got out of the taxi, that he should look up to see it, directly in front of him, out the airport window.

It was obvious, however, that there was going to be a confrontation when he returned with the "higher authority" in the form of a stocky police sergeant in his forties and a "Barney Fife" type police corporal. Ron had filed a report with these same men earlier and now updated them. The sergeant was interested to hear the taxi driver's story as the three of them approached the taxi where the driver, still in the taxi, and the female security guard waited.

"What's the problem here?" asked the broad-shouldered policeman.

"This man has my money," said Ron.

Ron gave them the explanation, yet again, of how he had left his wallet in this particular cab and that he had already called the cab company.

"Get out of the car," said the senior officer to the driver.

Ron went on to give details that only he would have known about the money the man had in his pocket.

"The $100 bills and the $20 bills would have a sharp two-crease fold," he explained. "I keep larger bills folded in a separate compartment of my wallet," he finished.

The authorities then looked at the cab driver, indicating it was his turn to speak.

"He's lying. It's my Christmas money for my kids!" barked the driver.

The lead policeman then asked Ron to step away from the potential confrontation in order to speak privately.

"Sir, it's like this," he began. "It's your word against his, and I really have no authority to tell him to give you the money," he said, clearly attempting to weasel out of the situation.

"Barney," who had until then remained calm and silent, suddenly came alive. Actually, he totally took over! He fast-stepped over to the driver and with confidence and authority said in a commanding tone, "Empty your pockets and put everything on the hood of the car!"

Totally stunned by the severity of the command, the driver responded. In just seconds there were three $100 bills and five $20 bills on the hood of the car along with other personal items. Not surprisingly, the bills had sharp two-fold creases in them, just as Ron had described.

"There they are, just as the man said," declared the junior authority pointing to the cash while looking at his partner. The evidence was undeniable thanks to one man who was not afraid to step forward and do the right thing.

The police officers took the taxi driver and Ron to their office. They called the taxi company and told them to send someone with authority to their office. Upon hearing the story, the driver was fired on the spot. After writing a detailed account of the entire incident, the money was returned to Ron. The "bold" officer persuaded the driver to lead him to the place he had thrown the wallet out the window and it also was retrieved and given back to Ron. The only money missing was $5 that the man had spent for lunch. Ron had to book a new flight, having missed the one he was supposed to be on during his search.

Only an hour and a half earlier, Ron had walked away from a cab leaving his wallet behind. Ron will admit there came a time when he had all but lost hope of finding his wallet and the money. How in the world in a town of hundreds of cabs and hundreds of miles of road in Louisville had Ron been able to locate that cab? Well, Ron is a man of faith who believes that everything is in God's hands.

Having reported the loss to the taxi company, the airport officials and the police and still experiencing no resolution, Ron took his case to the "highest authority." There he stood in the terminal in front of a big window feeling dejected and angry about what had just happened. Ron was bent over looking at the floor, feeling incredibly dejected and, frankly, angry with God. Nonetheless, it was to God he boldly spoke.

"Lord, how could you let this happen to me?" he began. "You know that every penny of that $400 has been tithed (10% to the church) on. You shouldn't have let Satan take it away from me." He was reminding God of His promise in the Bible to provide for those who honor Him with their tithe.

No sooner had those words come out of Ron's mouth than he

looked up from the floor and out the window to see "the" taxi, and the driver who had driven off with his wallet, parked right in front of him!

The Story of the Story

If the name Ron Mandich sounds familiar, there is good reason. Ron was also featured in "From Another Plane." We got this story at the same time as that one. Just like the other, there's a great sermon if you look for it. Ron said that he prays for that taxi driver every time he thinks of this story and he is trusting that God used this episode to turn the taxi driver's life around. If it hasn't happened yet, perhaps he will read this account and it will happen then.

A Box Full of Miracles

Times were not good for Bryan Semrow, 30, and his two and one-half-year-old son, Jordan, in January of 1993. Bryan's wife and Jordan's mother, Nita, had just died of breast cancer, leaving them with only each other. As if things weren't tough enough, their insurance company had reneged on paying Nita's medical bills, forcing Bryan to sell virtually everything they owned just to make ends meet. This included liquidating their home, land, and other interests.

With literally no savings or other valuable assets left, Bryan's mom encouraged him and Jordan to come to live with her until they could get back on their feet. Bryan secured a job at Jack's Pizza. He also chose to return to the fellowship at his former church after four years of "backsliding." Bryan would be the first to admit that for too long he tried to do things without God's help or counsel. Now things were getting pretty rough and Bryan knew he needed divine intervention to not only help him get through the grief process, but to get back on his feet financially.

Bryan's job was quite monotonous. Big dough balls plopped onto a conveyer belt as a hot press stamped out four pizza crusts at a time. One night as a dough ball dropped, a Bible verse landed into Bryan's spirit. It was from Genesis. *"Get out of your country, from your family, and from your father's house, to a land that I will show you."* Bryan's first thought was this meant God was leading him to go to Bible College in Twin Peaks, California.

Bryan had decided against going to Bible College years earlier. At that time, he had no intention of following God's leading, especially if it meant he'd have to go to California. California may not have been "foreign" in the classic sense, but he had never been there, so it qualified as a "foreign land" as far as he was concerned.

Now things were different.

That evening after work, Bryan went home and spoke to his mother, Janet, about the possibility of going off to college. Another verse came to his mind that evening from the book of Joshua. "*Have I not commanded you? Be strong and of good courage, do not be afraid, or be dismayed, for the Lord your God is with you wherever you go.*" Bright and early the very next morning his mother called out to Bryan.

"Bryan, look at this!" she said pointing at her "verse of the day" calendar.

It was from Joshua 1:9, the same verse that he had been given divinely just the night before! Bryan felt confirmed in his decision. It would take courage to pack up his and Jordan's belongings and leave everything they knew to head to the west coast, but the timing was right. He contacted a Bible school in Twin Peaks, California, and applied for acceptance there. Bryan would need money for tuition. Probate court was still determining Nita's estate, so no financial settlement had yet been determined. As sole survivor, he would certainly receive something. The question was, "How much?"

One day in December of 1993, Bryan made his routine exam of his mailbox. On this day, however, nothing would be usual or routine. In a stack of bills and junk mail were two letters. One was a letter of acceptance to Bible school. The other was an envelope with a letter from Probate that included a check for $5,000 from Nita's estate. Though grateful, Bryan knew that the money received would never be sufficient to get him through the next couple of years of tuition and raising Jordan. Still, the letters were a "sign" as far as Bryan was concerned. It was time to pack and go to Bible school to pursue becoming a pastor, a calling that he had shunned years earlier.

Bryan hugged his mom and said goodbye. Jordan blew her kisses and off they went to California in Bryan's 1978 Jeep CJ7. He had been told earlier in the week by four mechanics that it wouldn't make it to the border of Illinois, much less to California. After six days, he and Jordan not only made it to California, but the Jeep ran for a couple more years without any problems.

Once Bryan paid his tuition, very little was left to live on. The father-son duo could not live in the less expensive dorms because school policy did not allow families to live on campus, so they had to rent an apartment. Fortunately, many fellow students took turns watching Jordan, which minimized daycare costs. God was watching over them day by day in other ways, too. One particular day changed Bryan's life and faith forever.

Bryan and Jordan got up and made a breakfast of the little that was left in the house refrigerator. Bryan showered. He was applying Old Spice Fresh Scent stick deodorant when he "hit plastic." The stick was virtually empty. In that moment of frustration he chose to pray.

"Lord, within the next couple of days, You'll have to provide the $2.00 I need to buy a stick of Old Spice Fresh Scent deodorant— unless, of course, You want me to stink!"

He then proceeded off to school with Jordan in tow. On the way there, Bryan decided to stop at a local gas station/convenience store to check his savings account balance through the ATM. While standing at the ATM, Jordan wandered into a toy section and found something he wanted.

"Daddy, can I have this?" he pleaded from across the room.

"I'm sorry, buddy, but daddy can't afford to get that for you right now," Bryan lamented.

Jordan had found a simple hand-held paddle game involving two Velcro-covered discs and a tennis ball. It only cost $3.00, but the bad news was the ATM screen clearly indicated that the savings account was nearly empty. There would be very little to live on, much less to buy a toy for Jordan. Bryan gathered up Jordan in his arms and off to daycare and school they went, a student-dad and a disappointed little three-year-old boy.

From the moment Bryan ran out of deodorant to the time he reached the school parking lot did not total more than fifteen minutes. Jordan had been delivered safely to his babysitter's home and Bryan arrived in the campus parking lot shortly after. It was semester break, and Bryan was scheduled to do some painting while the campus was empty. Clearly no one was around. His Jeep was the only one in the parking lot. He grabbed his Walkman from the back seat and headed toward school.

After walking only thirty yards, he realized that he had taken the wrong cassette tape to listen to. He turned and walked back to his vehicle. As he approached the driver's door he noticed something sitting in clear view on the seat. Not a soul was to be seen, but he could feel something was going on.

There, sitting on the front seat of the Jeep, was a box. A white envelope was taped to the top. Written on the card was, "To Bryan, from God." Below that was a verse, Matthew 6:33, *"But seek first the kingdom of God and His righteousness, and all these things shall be added unto you."*

Bryan opened the envelope. It contained a $100 bill. Tears filled his eyes as he realized God had answered his prayer for funds. However, there was more in the box. He looked down upon three sticks of Old Spice Fresh Scent deodorant. Apparently God was making a point of *not* wanting him to stink! Then he noticed one more gift nestled underneath the deodorant. It was a handheld paddle game that included two Velcro-covered discs and a tennis ball!

The Story of the Story

Bryan told Steve this story in person. We would find it absolutely incredible if we both had not been the recipients of a few miracles ourselves, and hadn't also know of many others who also have experienced similar Godincidences.

Today, Bryan is a pastor and he is doing very well. He and Jordan are no longer alone. On July 20, 1996, he married a wonderful woman by the name of Jane.

Bryan made a comment while telling Steve this story that has stayed with both of us. He said, "You know, my wife is working and I am a pastor. We have ample income. Now, miracles don't happen on that scale anymore. Today, the provision of the Lord is through small, daily miracles. He is still our Provider, but that doesn't mean that it has to be through such dramatic means. He made His point over and over again while at school that He is in control, and now I am willing to trust Him always."

What a wonderful revelation.

Meet Me in the Airport

If it had happened only once, perhaps even twice, there might have been a discussion of the possibility of a coincidence, but when it happens three or four times? I'm referring to the frequent, unexpected guest that has "appeared" to Nora Holzwart. Nora loves to share her story of a special person who has a knack for showing up, no matter where she's at or what part of the country she's in.

By her own admission, Nora was a rebel without a cause when she found herself as a witness for her friend Pam's wedding. It was the summer of 1983. The setting was Calvary Chapel, a rather odd place to Nora. For starters, the last time she was there the building was a motorcycle dealership. It was a peculiar kind of church to her in that it had no stain glass windows, they played music with guitars, and the man doing the service was not in a black robe. His name was Dwight Douville, who gave his life to Christ during the Jesus Movement of the early '70s, now turned pastor.

As Nora stood there at her friend's wedding, she found herself feeling angry and jealous. She was about to lose her friend. But as the minister spoke, something broke in Nora's spirit. Little did she know that her life would be changed forever. In a moment, something swept over Nora that turned her anger and disappointment into love, so much so that she felt compelled to talk with Pastor Douville. As she sat on the church pew after the service, she felt much like a deer in headlights.

"Wanna tell me about what happened to you during the wedding?" questioned Dwight gently.

"Wow, I'm not sure, but it's nice," she confessed.

After the party at Carter Park, Pam, Gary and Nora went to

Pastor Douville's and his wife Jane's home to sign the marriage papers. It was then that Pastor explained that Nora had indeed had a spiritual encounter with the Lord. She quickly called a friend who had been praying for her to experience the love of God.

Fast forward to the late '90s. Nora was quite candid about the fact that she was not in a good place in her faith. Frankly, she had become the captain of her own ship and had not allowed God to have any part in her daily decisions. It showed. Then, on a bet from a friend, a professional football player with the Green Bay Packers, Nora dared to commit her life back to God. She did, but felt she was in spiritual crisis and needed some accountability from her friends to stay in a good place with God. That, however, required her to be real, which was a frightening concept to Nora. It would mean not only living out her faith day to day, but sharing her faith with others as opportunities arose. She decided it was time to make her commitment real.

One of the outreach ministries of Calvary Chapel is a restaurant called Pilgrim's Café. It was there that Nora began to share her story of how her life changed through the renewing power of God's love.

One noon hour, as she was sharing her story with a friend, Nora mentioned that Dwight Douville had played a special role in her past. At the moment she was talking about him, he walked in! Not that big a deal in that it's a part of the church, if you will, but nonetheless "God timing."

Forward to circa 2002 in Chicago's O'Hare Airport. Maybe you've had the joy (or misery) of being part of the masses that flow through the airport. Nora was there doing what she does best, and that's talk about her faith, even with complete strangers. That's precisely what she was doing while walking between terminals.

"My life changed one summer night in 1983," she explained. At the moment she was telling her story to a man, it happened again. The words were still coming out of her mouth.

"Many times when I'm telling people about Pastor Douville,

he unexpectedly shows up," she told the man. "As a matter of fact, there he is now," she pointed, in an excited tone, as if he had been cued to appear.

Yes, Dwight Douville had appeared out of nowhere at O'Hare Airport in Chicago at the precise moment she spoke his name! How many people walk through that place in any given day over a 24-hour period, maybe ten thousand? Thousands and thousands? Well, you get the idea.

"Aw, that's just a coincidence," the man said.

"No, it's a 'God-thing,'"said Nora grinning for ear to ear.

Fast-forward yet again to June of 2004. A tired Dwight Douville could barely think straight after a day of air travel from the west coast. He landed in the Minneapolis-St. Paul Airport. Because he lives in Appleton, he just assumed he would be flying there. So he found that gate. He arrived in plenty of time to relax for a bit and do some reading. Dwight received a jolt as he gave his ticket to the flight attendant who was boarding the passengers.

"Sir, you're at the wrong gate. This is the Appleton bound gate. You are heading to Green Bay!" she informed him. "That flight is leaving in 15 minutes!"

Dwight realized that he would have to have to hurry to make his connection.

Dwight prayed as he ran to find a tram to rush him to the Green Bay gate. Time was limited. Suddenly he saw a tram coming toward him. Remarkably, it slowed down and then stopped right in front of him. As he stepped into the tram, he realized that going to the other gate was *not* a mistake after all. For standing right in front of him was Nora Holzwart and her friend, Kelly Backus. Nora had told Kelly just minutes earlier on their return flight from Alaska about Pastor Dwight Douville's uncanny ability to show up after she referred to him in conversations!

The Story of the Story

"It's the Lord, Nora," were Pastor Douville's first words to Nora when he saw her in the tram. She didn't need to be convinced. Dwight's unexpected appearances have deepened Nora's faith incredibly.

A Passing Glass

The Kartos family is no different than most others. They love good conversations and good meals. Meet Tom and Nancy and their children, Tanya and Molly. It's November of 1995 as they invite you into the dining room of their modest middle American home. The menu for the evening features baked fish, au gratin potatoes and corn with all the trimmings.

The "aroma of the sea" had already wafted throughout their home when Mom declared supper ready.

"Tanya, can you get the fish from the oven, please."

"Sure," she replied obediently.

Using a spatula, Tanya gently put the flaky fish on a platter. She then set the nine-by-thirteen inch glass baking dish down on top of the stove. From there she carried the platter into the dining room that was located just off of the kitchen.

As they enjoyed the fine food, the family talked about the day, how school was for the girls, how work was for Dad. Mom managed to get a few words in also. While the family ate and conversed, an unusual crackling sound seemed to come from the kitchen. Initially, Nancy ignored it until finally the noise became more intense.

"What is that?" asked Nancy.

"What's what?" asked Tom as he continued to eat.

Few people would argue that God gives to women intuitive gifts. In this case, Nancy simply "knew" she needed to get into the kitchen. She looked over at the stove and discovered that one of the burners on the stove had been kept on low heat. What was of more concern was that she saw the baking pan sitting on top of it.

"Oh, no! Oh, my goodness!" said Nancy.

The crackling was coming from the glass pan, which was cooking with nothing inside it. It had been slowly heating all through dinner.

Nancy knew she had to move it, immediately! She grabbed an oven mitt from the drawer and reached over to quickly remove the pan from the stove's surface. As she reached for it, standing only inches from the pan, the dish exploded into thousands of tiny pieces, peppering the kitchen!

There were glass chards embedded in the counter. There were glass chards embedded in the floor. The force had blown pieces of glass underneath the microwave and into the carpet in the dining room. It had melted the counter top and the floor in the places it landed. (They both would have to be replaced.) The only area that appeared to have been spared was about a 16-inch diameter area on the floor where Nancy had been standing. Nancy couldn't help but note that something quite extraordinary had occurred. She reviewed, with incredulousness, what had just happened. She looked to each side of her and there was glass everywhere. She looked behind her, and there was glass everywhere. The observation begged a good question.

"How had the thousands of burning, sharp projectiles gotten behind her without passing through her, or even touching her?"

Candy for Rainee

The Breddas were preparing to move to Savannah, Georgia. Little three-year-old Rainee loved to play in the park just a house down from them on the end of the block. Rainee had begun to play on the merry-go-round when an elderly man with grayish-brown hair in a tweed jacket came up to her and struck up a conversation.

"Hi, sweetheart. How would you like to get some candy?" he asked.

"Yeah!" she answered back to the seemingly kind man.

"The candy is at my house," he told Rainee. "You'll have to come with me," he said with a smile.

He grabbed the tiny girl's hand and they began to leave as Rainee anticipated a treat. The man's house apparently was just down the street from the Breddas. Just as they stepped onto the sidewalk, another much younger man grabbed Rainee's free hand and spoke to her.

"You need to ask your father if getting some candy is okay," he said in a kind, but authoritative voice.

Rainee held both men's hands until she arrived at the sidewalk of her home. Then she let go of the old man's hand and began to run to her house that was only a few feet away, still holding the hand of the second man. Quickly the young girl was talking to her dad who was standing right by the front door in the hall.

"Can I go and get some candy at that man's house?" she said as she pointed at the elderly gentleman who'd made the initial invitation.

Mr. Bredda glanced toward the man who had already turned to run away and, like a rocket, the protective dad ran out of the house in pursuit of the man who had now taken off running across the street. He did catch him very quickly. He grabbed the elderly man by the shirt and began to yell at him.

The little tyke was confused by what was happening, but she was also baffled because the second man had somehow mysteriously vanished. When her father came back she asked him a simple question.

"Daddy, are you mad at the other man, too?"

Mr. Bredda had absolutely no idea what his daughter was talking about. The only man he had seen was an old man – the one he had just run out of the neighborhood!

The Story of the Story

Rainee told her dad that the other man had a nice face and blond hair. Her dad again assured her there was only the elderly man that he had confronted.

Still, we know that God often sends a "messenger" to care for a little one who's facing potential danger. Just ask Rainee (Bredda) Booher.

"Look What I Found!"

"What have we just done?" wondered Pastor Arni Jacobson.

This is the question that was going through Arni's mind as he and his wife, Jan, drove home from church. It was the winter of 1983. Pastor Jacobson had just returned from a missions conference where the participants had been urged to step out in faith and make a financial contribution to the cause of world missions.

On that particular Sunday, Arni stood in the pulpit of the church he was pastoring, Salt Lake Christian Center, and encouraged his own congregation to make the same "faith pledge" to the work of missions as he had done earlier at the conference by modeling a commitment himself. His hope was to inspire them to the same level of commitment he made.

"Jan and I would like to pledge $200 per month for the next twelve months to this cause," Pastor Arni professed publicly. "We urge you to pray about it, and then make a pledge on behalf of your family as well," he finished.

The pledge they had just made was more than an honorable gesture given the fact that the family, which included Arni, Jan and their five-year-old son Chad, had just recently answered "the call" to move from a similar-sized congregation in Merrill, where they had been pastoring.

It's worth noting that property values, translated "housing costs," were about 30% higher in Salt Lake than in the Midwest. Though living expenses were greater, Arni's salary was nearly the same as before. Thus, the math revealed it might not have been the wisest idea in "man's economy" for the Jacobsons to make such a commitment.

Over lunch, Jan and Arni discussed how they would be able to keep their promise. As a matter of fact, they wondered if they had truly heard from the Lord on the matter.

"Did we do the right thing?" Arni asked Jan.

"Yes, we did, honey," she said affirming her husband's expression of faith. "God *will* provide," she assured.

Over their years in ministry together the couple had watched God do so many miraculous things to provide for them. They chose not to be in a panic over the pledge. However, they did intend to make their first installment on the pledge at the Sunday evening service, which was only hours away, and they both knew that the checkbook was "thin."

While Arni and Jan relaxed that afternoon, young Chad had energy to burn, so he spent time playing outdoors with friends for a while. After he returned home later that afternoon he went upstairs to his room to read. On his bookshelf were about fifteen small Bible story children's books. He reached for one, plopped himself down on the bed and began to read.

Just hours before the evening service, Chad came downstairs to show mom and dad something he had discovered while reading that afternoon.

"Mom and dad, look what I found!" he said.

Arni and Jan could only smile as they looked at one another with a heart full of delight and amazement at how God had chosen to honor their pledge. Nestled between two pages in one of Chad's books were two, crisp $100 bills!

The Story of the Story

This was just the first of many ways that God faithfully provided the $200 needed each month to fulfill the Jacobson's pledge. To this day neither Arni nor Jan recall ever putting that money in Chad's book. What they do recall, however, is how that experience helped to build not only their faith, but Chad's as well.

Floating on Flames of Mercy

Sunday, August 8, 2004, time for the Tillman's yearly adventure to Crescent Lake Bible Camp in the northern woods of Rhinelander. When we say adventure, we mean adventure. Mark and Sue have more than a family, they constitute a tiny village! Packed into the fifteen-passenger 1989 Ford Econoline van, besides mom and dad, were children Tristan, Jeff, Isaac, Katie, Jonah, Nathaniel, Jimmy, Dustin, and granddaughter, Breanna.

As the van pulled out of the driveway of their Neenah home Tristan piped up from the back.

"We need to pray for safe travels."

"You're right, honey," said Sue. She glanced at Mark, who took her cue immediately.

"Dear Lord, we thank you for what you have done for this family. We pray for traveling mercies. We ask all of this in the name of Jesus, Amen," he finished.

The van became a "riding party" as the kids played, talked, giggled, and had a great time. The first two hours of the trip was uneventful. As they approached US Highway 51, near Tomahawk, however, Mark began to notice a "pulling and tugging" while steering the van.

"Mark, why don't you pull off at the next exit and see what's the matter?" suggested Sue.

At first Mark balked at the idea, not wanting to lose travel time, but then he conceded it was probably a good idea. They found a small gas station a bit further down the highway and pulled in. Mark and Tristan got out to search for problems. Initially, they did not find anything wrong. Then Mark pulled off a hubcap.

"Oh, my word!" yelled Mark, kneeling by the edge of the tire.

Sue hopped from the van to see what Mark was making all the fuss about. She couldn't believe her eyes. All eight lug nuts on the left front tire were loose. More than that, the lug nut holes in the rim were actually egg-shaped! There was no way that the lug nuts could be tightened. The threads were too worn. Even if the lug nuts themselves had not been damaged, there was no real-sized hole to which they could be anchored. Mark took stock of the situation before making a determination.

"I think we'll be able to make it the rest of the way," he said confidently looking at Sue, who wasn't quite as assured.

"If you think so," she said skeptically.

They hopped back into the van to rejoin their waiting children. In no time they were back on US Highway 51 heading north going 55-mph. A short time later they turned on Highway 8-East. It was nearing dusk when Katie called out from the back.

"I smell smoke!"

"No, you don't, honey. I'm sure it's not smoke, just something that smells like it," Sue retorted, trying to bring a calm to the family. Katie wasn't buying it, however.

"Yes, I do! I really do!"

Suddenly Sue smelled it, too. Fear began to well up inside, and Sue was having a difficult time not letting the children see it.

"Honey, maybe we better pull over. Something feels very strange, like we're floating, or we're in a boat," said Sue who was feeling quite concerned.

"It does, doesn't it?" Mark agreed.

No sooner had the words come out of Sue's mouth when Mark had a very clear sense that he'd better pull over, now! As he reached the shoulder of the road, they heard a loud "pop" from the rear. When they got out, they discovered the back right tire had completely blown. Shredded rubber lay all over the road behind them.

Sue and Tristan walked to the nearest house to make a phone call to summon a tow truck while Mark stayed behind with the rest of the crew. Within a half-hour a tow truck arrived. The service man from the towing company circled the van in utter amazement before speaking.

"How in the dickens did you not flip this van?" he said. "There's no way that you should have been able to drive this rig with the rear tire in that condition, not to mention the looks of those front lug nuts. Good

Lord, man!"

The repairman helped change the tires. Soon the Tillmans were back on the road, arriving at camp just a bit late. The following morning Mark took the van to a local garage to be thoroughly checked. They fixed the lug nuts on the front tire, provided a new spare and the rest of the trip was wonderfully uneventful.

Early the next week, Mary Svitavsky, a friend of Mark's and Sue's friends, Harry and Sue Kratz, asked Sue Kratz a question.

"How are the Tillmans doing?"

"Doin' fine as far as I know," she told Mary.

The Tillmans had already shared with the Kratzs the details of their "journey" from the weekend before.

"Why do you ask?" she quizzed.

"Well, I was kind of concerned, really," she said. "This past Saturday night I had a dream about them and their family. I dreamed I was following their van in my car when, without warning, the right rear tire blew out and shredded all over the road. The van was traveling about 55 mph. It went into the ditch and rolled several times. I got out of my car and ran over to their van. I looked inside and saw a bunch of kids." She then paused, hesitating as to how to finish. "And half of them were dead."

The Story of the Story

Steve met Mark Tillman at a business meeting. Shortly after that, he met Sue and a few of the children and quickly became fascinated with their role as foster parents. It's a "calling" to do what they do. Many of their foster children have special needs. We have Sarah, also a special needs child. Having Sarah has helped us develop an even greater compassion and admiration for others who are raising kids with special challenges.

When Steve visited the Tillman's home for the first time, he shared a few of the stories from this book. Sue was especially riveted.

Steve visited again two weeks later in June. He was sitting with the clan eating some chicken strips when Sue told him this story. Until then, it hadn't truly totally hit either her or Mark just how serious a disaster may have been averted on August 8, 2004. When we helped them to connect the dots, both Sue and Mark sat in amazement of God's intervention.

We sincerely believe that if God would not have intervened, Mary Svitavsky's dream may have been prophetic. It's worth noting that Mary had the dream on August 7th, the night before the Tillman's trip!

Mark and Sue are currently caring for 11 children at Haven Homes of the Valley, their Foster Care/Respite Home. They are truly an amazing couple.

Goodbye for Now

Scott Marciniak loved to ride his bike. On the 4th of July in 1976, he and some friends embarked on a 50-mile journey on the busy holiday-packed roads. As he rode away his mother, Toni, prayed.

"Lord, please protect him. I know I cannot, but You can."

The guys returned home safely from the trip.

Scott was a very bright boy who graduated at 17-years old in 1978. He was good-looking and well liked. He was a gifted musician who had been in band since he was 15. Scott had plenty of hopes and dreams for what appeared to be a bright future.

On the 23rd of June, just two weeks after he graduated, a friend picked him up. They picked up another friend and all three young men headed for High Cliff Park.

"Goodbye, Scott," said Toni to her son as she watched him drive away.

Toni went to a "home party" at her neighbor's home. It broke up earlier than she had expected. As she left to go home, she heard sirens. Toni began to pray for those involved in the emergency as was, and still is, her practice. Upon arriving home, she turned on the police band radio and heard all the details of the accident. It had involved teen-aged boys.

Apparently, three young men were headed out of town when an oncoming vehicle swerved into their lane and hit them head on, killing all three. The couple in the car that had crossed the centerline had only minor injuries.

Later that evening came the horrifying news that one of the dead boys was her son, Scott. Toni had given her heart to the Lord just years earlier, so she knew from Whom to gather her strength. Her brother, who had been at a prayer meeting, came home and told Toni he felt that she was supposed to take comfort in the Bible passage from Psalms 39. In this portion of Scripture David expresses how deeply troubled he is by the fragility of life.

Toni took great comfort in knowing Scott had made a choice to trust in the Lord about a year before the accident that took his life. That brought her some peace and comfort. In the following weeks during the challenges of grieving Scott, Toni had asked God a few times to assure her that her son was safe. She said she would only ask Him one more time.

A few weeks later, a friend's mother died. Toni went to look through a collection of cards she kept in a box in the living room. She knelt down on the floor, picked up the box and opened it. The very first card on top of the pile was a handmade card that she had never used because she just didn't know to whom she would send such a card. Toni remained on her knees and shed tears of comfort, thanking the Lord for His faithfulness.

The inside of the greeting card Toni had opened read, "At the gates of heaven, a child waits to welcome you."

The Story of the Story

Although this is the last of the stories in this book, it's not the last word. Read on...

One Last Word

By Kathi Rose

Neither Steve nor I would ever want to minimize the importance of divine intervention in the lives of men, nor do we want to analyze why miracles do or don't happen. Sometimes people exercise their faith, believe and then receive miracles. Miracles can encourage our faith in God. Others who profess to have no faith have also been the recipients of a miracle. As a result, they have come to faith. Both Steve and I have been the recipients of incredible grace and mercy, both in miraculous ways as well as in the every day goodness of a benevolent God.

Having said that, I confess there were certain times that I had needed, prayed, even longed for a miracle, and it did not happen. So heartfelt was the longing that, when a miracle was not extended to me, I became angry....angry with a God I *knew* had the power to intervene but did not...angry with a God who I *knew* loved me yet, to my way of thinking, had let me down...angry with a God whose compassion for my plight seemed limited and unmovable.

You see, the *Baby on the Blanket* (p.24) was my son Nathan. Only a short 19 years later, he and his wife Jenny, both righteous, God-fearing young adults, would be killed in a motorcycle/truck accident. There would be no warning; there would be no angel; there would be no miracle; there would be no hope, at least not this side of eternity. Where was God while catastrophe was pillaging my life? Does God not keep watch over His children both day and night? Is it possible that God actually "blinks" from time to time? Why save Nathan once, but not twice?

Perhaps you, too, have felt anger at the seeming randomness of God's intervention in the lives of men. Perhaps you've asked yourself the same questions I asked. Perhaps you still wonder, still feel angry, and still have no resolution. Or, perhaps this book has "stirred" in you a renewed passion for answers to such questions.

I do not pretend to have answers to such divine enigmas, but there are a few certainties by which I now live my life that may prove to be helpful to you, as well.

God is a good and loving God. He has a plan for each of our lives; a plan not to harm us, but to give us a hope and a future. That plan includes a life beyond the grave, a home in heaven with Him through Jesus.

God is an incredible economist. He wastes nothing. When we are faced with the inevitabilities of human experience (divorce, unemployment, sickness or death, to name but a few), He will either deliver us *out* of them, or give us grace to pass *through* them. Either way, He will use what was intended for our destruction and, if we allow Him, He will use it for our good – to change us, to deepen us, to give us compassion, empathy, love and understanding for others' struggles. I have learned that it's not my circumstances, good or bad, that change me for better or worse, but rather it's how I choose to respond to my circumstances that will dictate who I am becoming.

God does *not* blink. He sees who we are. He sees what we most need. He sees the bigger picture. A small piece of the bigger picture for your life may simply be that you are reading this book right now, and deciding to receive God's love for you. If that is the case, you've just become the recipient of the greatest miracle of all!

Is that coincidence or Godincidence?

About Steve Rose

Steve Rose burst onto the scene in 1996 with the release of the best-selling book, *Leap of Faith: God Must Be A Packer Fan* (Angel Press of WI, Sept 1996), which sold more than 50,000 copies. He did a radio talk show with the Green Bay Packers in the '90s that birthed the book. He wrote two *Leap of Faith* sequels and a personal development book called *7 Steps from your Dreams to your Destiny*.

Steve, as well as being an author-speaker, has been involved in radio for over 25 years. He also hosted his own television show called the *Leap of Faith* TV Show on FOX-11 in Green Bay from 1998-1999.

Today, Steve and his wife, Kathi, own Winners Success Network, their speaking and publishing company. They are also a partner in a website development company called smallbizwebsolutions.biz where they build websites for businesses.

Steve is available to share his experiences and lessons in churches, schools and businesses of any size. His down-to-earth humorous style brings an important message of help, hope and encouragement. Steve shares how he has recovered from adversity and how others can, too.

About Kathi Rose

Kathi Rose has quite a personal story. Her book, *I Climbed a Mountain: A Mother's Diary of Tragedy, Grief & Triumph* (written under the name Kathi Pollard) has brought comfort to those who have gone through the grieving process. Besides having lost a child, Kathi is a breast cancer survivor and has raised a special-needs child.

Kathi is an ordained pastor on staff at her home church, Evangel Worship Center in Menasha, Wisconsin. She also ministers to women at Taycheedah Correctional Institution. Kathi has also worked for the Billy Graham Evangelistic Association.

Kathi does women's retreats and speaks on other topics of spiritual wholeness. She is available to speak to groups of any size or gender. She is one of the most eloquent speakers in the country. Kathi serves as President of *Leap of Faith Ministries*, a non-profit Evangelistic Outreach set up by her and her husband.

She and her husband, Steve, live in Neenah, Wisconsin with her daughter, Sarah.

Steve Rose speaking menu

The Greatest Leap of Faith Yet	(churches)
7 Steps from your Dreams to your Destiny	(companies, keynotes)
The Power of Purpose	(high schools & colleges)
FMO "For Men Only"	(men's groups & retreats)

Books by Steve Rose

Leap of Faith: God Must Be A Packer Fan	(1996, Angel Press of WI)
Leap of Faith 2: God Loves Packer Fans	(1997, Prairie Oak Press)
Leap of Faith 3: The Packer Hall of Faith	(1998, WSN Publishing)
7 Steps from Your Dreams to Your Destiny	(2001, WSN Publishing)

Kathi Rose speaking menu

Destined for Wholeness	(churches & retreats)
Principles to Gain & Maintain the Victory	(churches & retreats)
The Value of Brokenness	(churches & retreats)
How to Run the Race	(schools, churches, retreats)

Books by Kathi Rose

I Climbed a Mountain:
A Mother's Diary of Tragedy, Grief & Triumph (1996, Morris Publishing)

To book Steve or Kathi Rose for a speaking engagement, a book signing or to order author-autographed copies of their books go to

www.godincidencebook.com

We love to hear stories of "Godincidences." If you have one you
would like to share with us go to our website.

www.godincidencebook.com